# PAINTINGS IN STYLE

## Art Exhibits

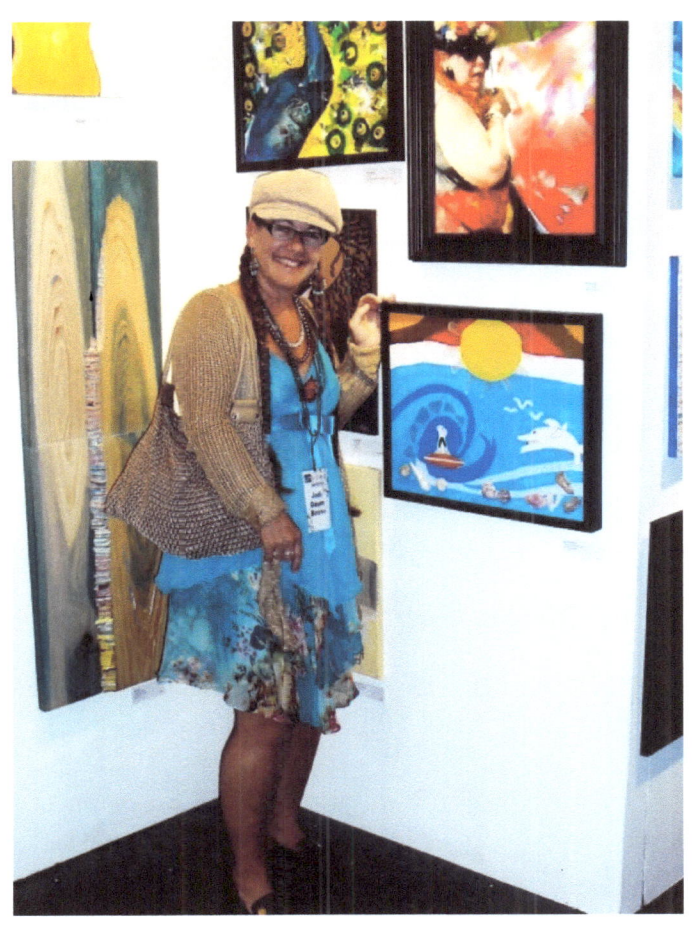

Jodi Daum Boone

Thank you for reading.  In the event that you
Appreciate this book, please consider sharing the
Good words by leaving a review, or connect with
the author.

Jodi Daum-Boone - Paintings
Peggy Leyva-Conley –
Editor, Book Layout, Photography

Printed in the United States of America

ISBN-13:  978-1536921007
ISBN-10:  1536921009

**Dedication**

To all the Artist of the World

# Table of Contents

Monthaven Art Society
Venue – Comer Mansion
Art Exhibit – Gallatin, Tennessee

Untitled – Naked Carnival
Venue – Diamond Sound Studios
Art Exhibit – Nashville, Tennessee

Untitled – The Island of Misfits
Venue – Building
Art Exhibit – Madison, Tennessee

Untitled Artist – Winter Show
Venue – East Gallery – Nashville, Tennessee
Art Exhibit

## About the Artist

Jodi Daum Boone was born in San Jose, California and raised in San Juan Bautista, California, San Benito County near the border of Monterey County on the Pacific Central Coastal region. She has lived in Ben Lomond in the Santa Cruz Mountains and on the Island of Maui. Included, Twain Harte, California in the High Sierra Mountains. She has continued to make her home in Hendersonville, Tennessee in the Old Hickory Lake area a suburb of Nashville, Tennessee.

At a young age, she began Painting, writing Poetry out in the Country inspired by Nature, People and places.

She is an International Musician (vocalist, guitarist) and is an Artist-Painter who specializes in Mediums of Acrylic, Watercolors, Pen and Mixed media. She has exhibited her Artwork in Galleries throughout parts of California and Tennessee.

Memberships have included the Monthaven Art Society, Hendersonville, Tennessee and Untitled Artist of Nashville, Tennessee.

The Author enjoys Boating, Swimming, Hiking, Walking and Bicycle riding.

She is a graduate of San Benito Joint Union High School, Hollister, California and attended Santa Cruz Beauty College in the field of Cosmetology. She also attended Gavilan College performing in Theatre Arts and music in Gilroy, California, Santa Clara County.

**Untitled**

**In Art We Trust**

Nashville, Tennessee

Exhibit - 2009

**Venue – Buffalo Billiards**

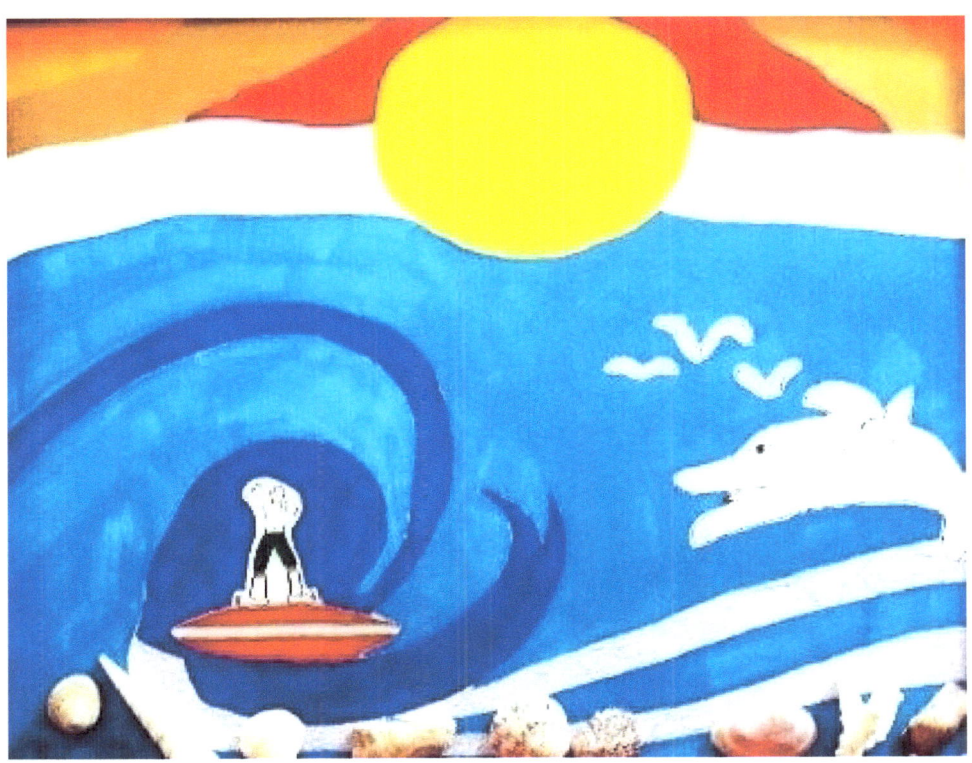

Acrylics - California Surfing

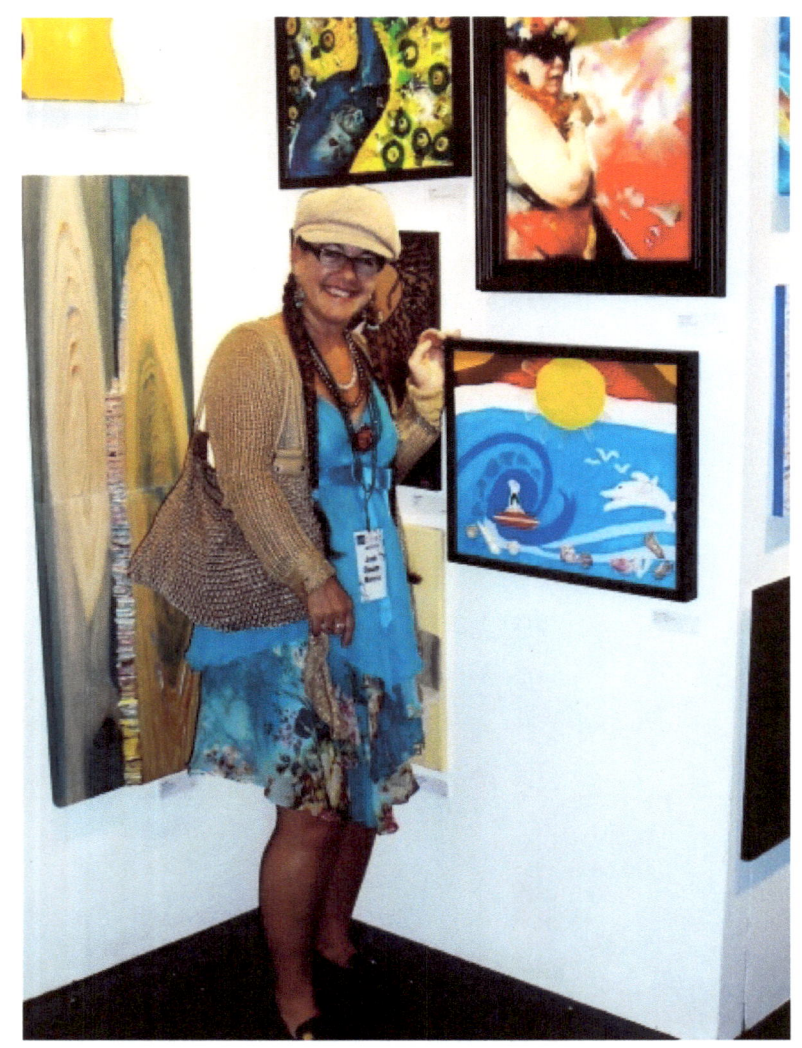

Vibrant Colors of paintings.

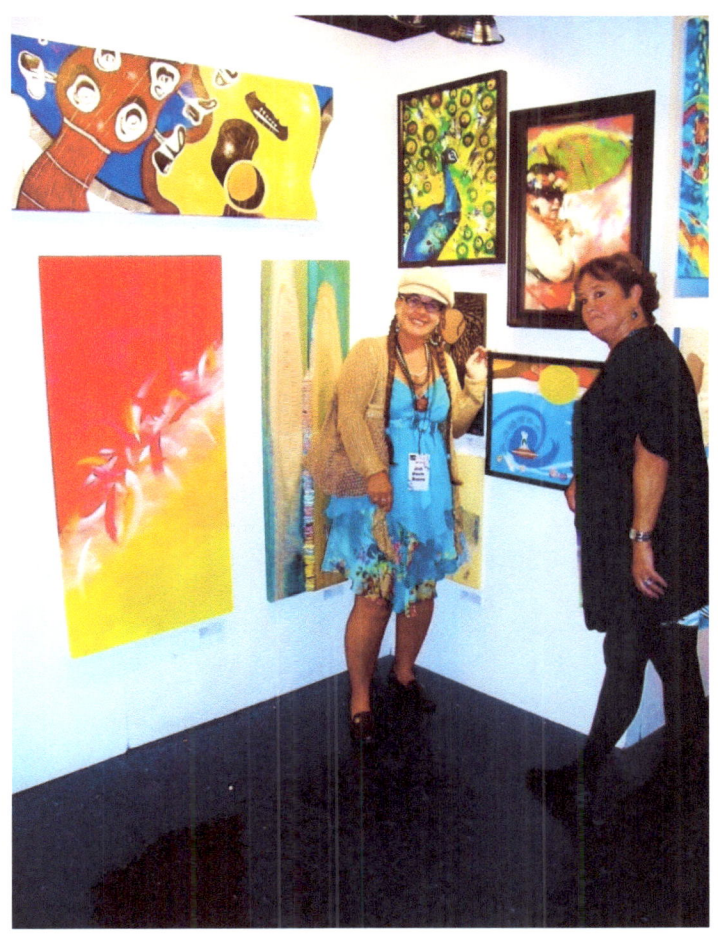

**Acrylics – California Surfing**

Jodi Daum Boone and Debbie Gilbert

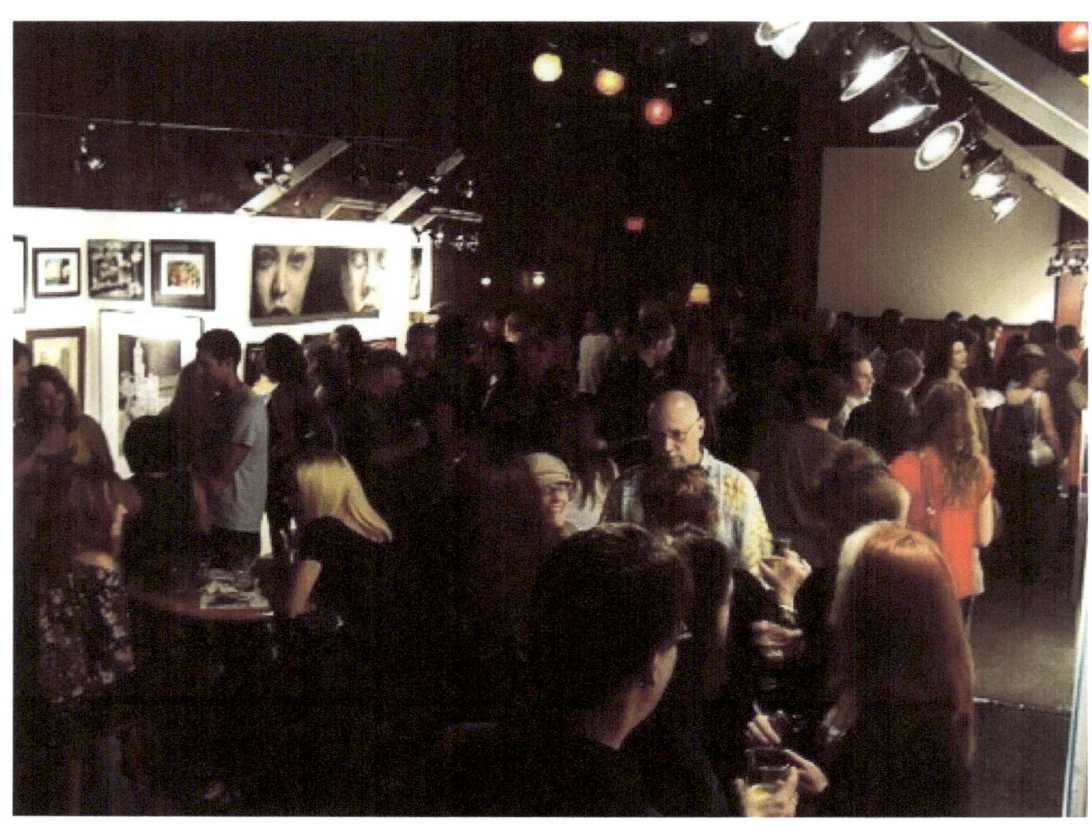

**Artist and Crowd**

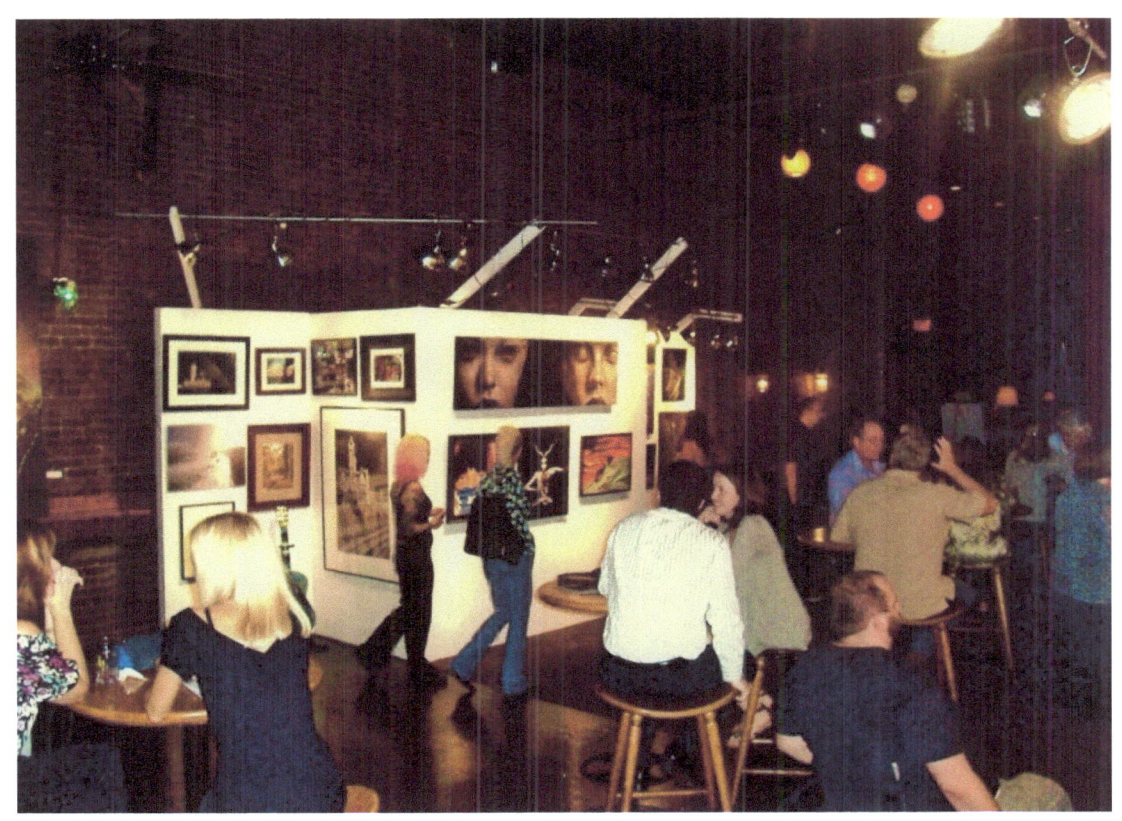

Art Panel – Paintings

Artist and Crowd

**Untitled**

**Barely Legal**

Nashville, Tennessee

**Venue – The Gulch**

Art Exhibit

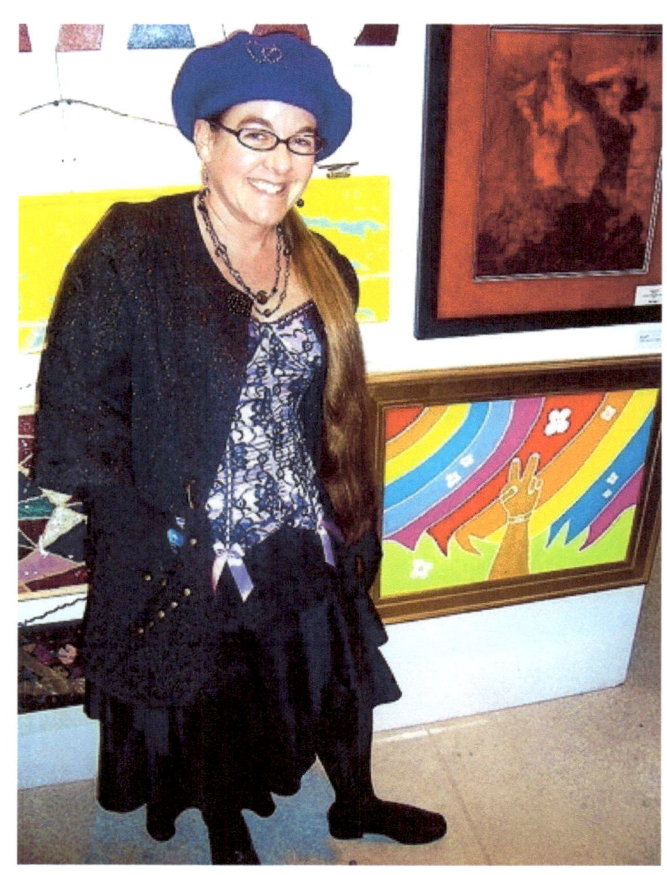

# Peace and Love

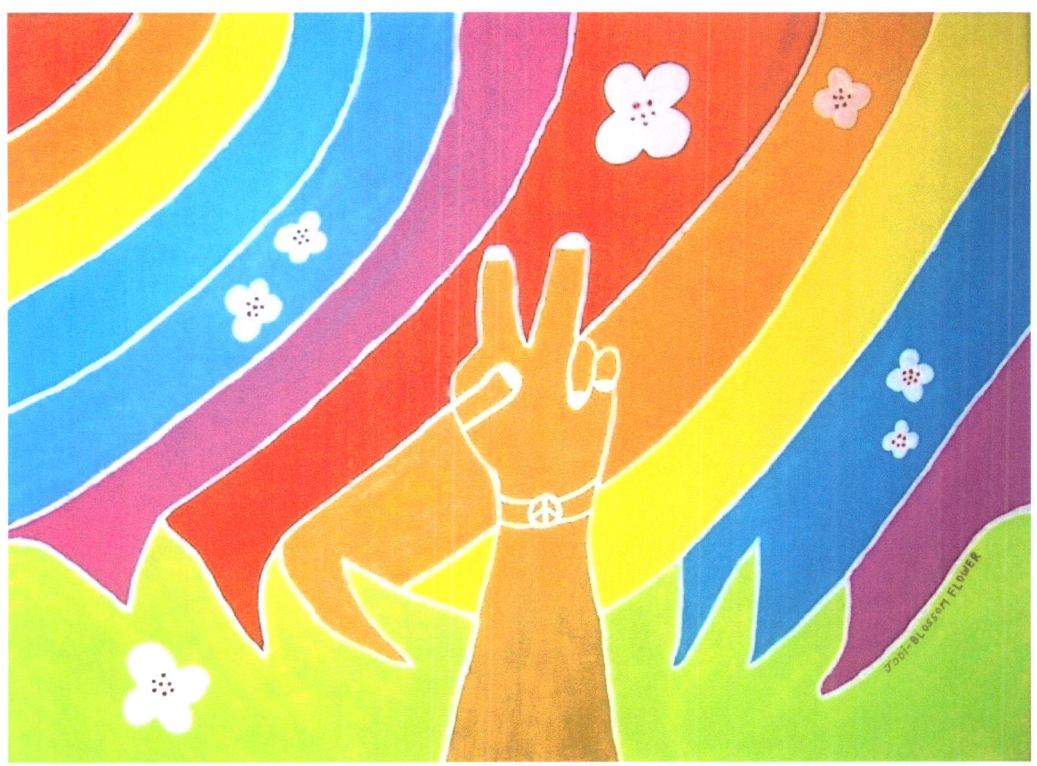

Acrylics

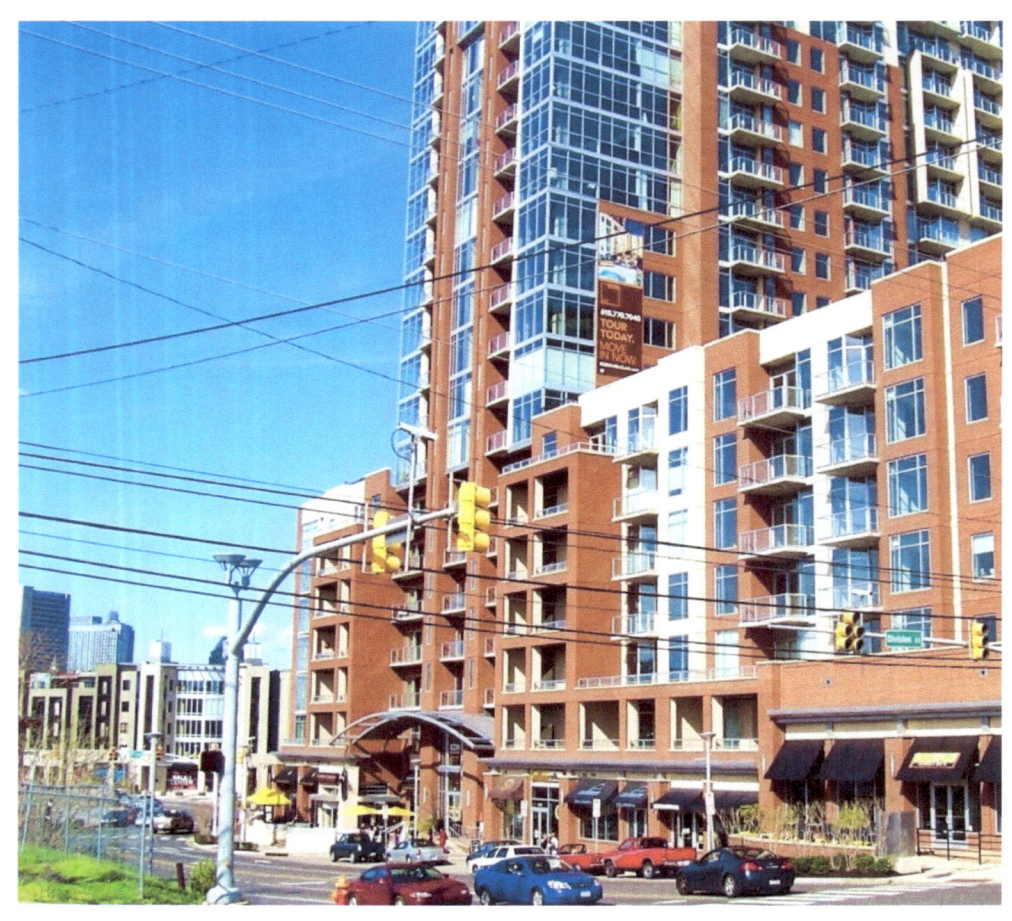

The Gulch – Nashville, Tennessee

**Untitled – Abominable**

Art Exhibit - 2013

**Venue – East Gallery**

Nashville, Tennessee

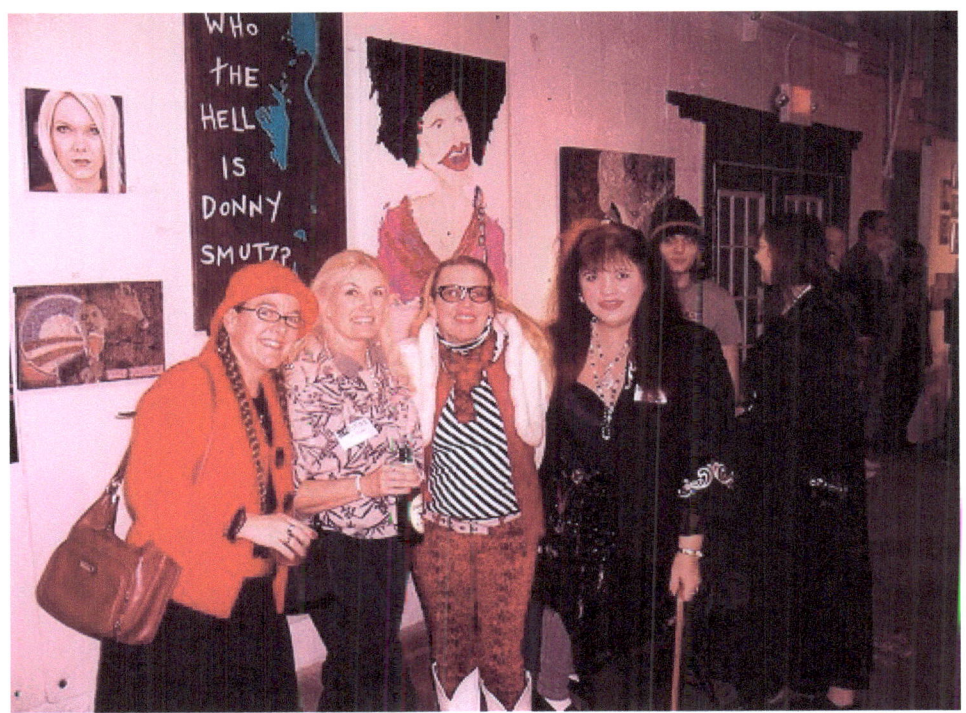

Left:  Jodi Daum Boone, Liz Stover, Von Derry, Peggy Leyva Conley

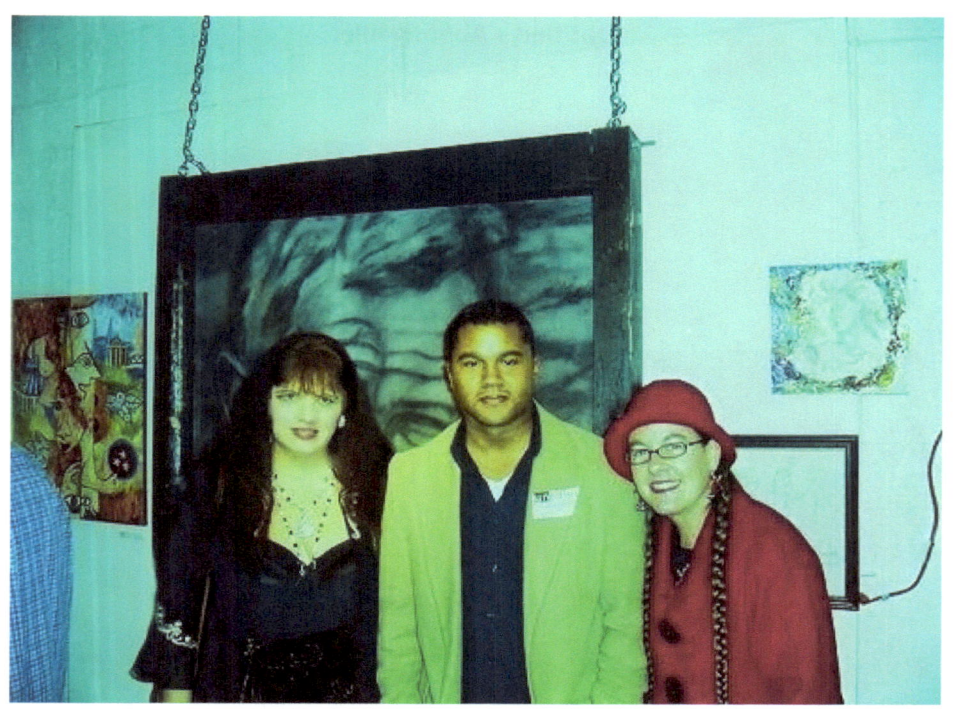

Artist Members

Peggy Leyva Conley, Stephen Watkins and Jodi Daum Boone

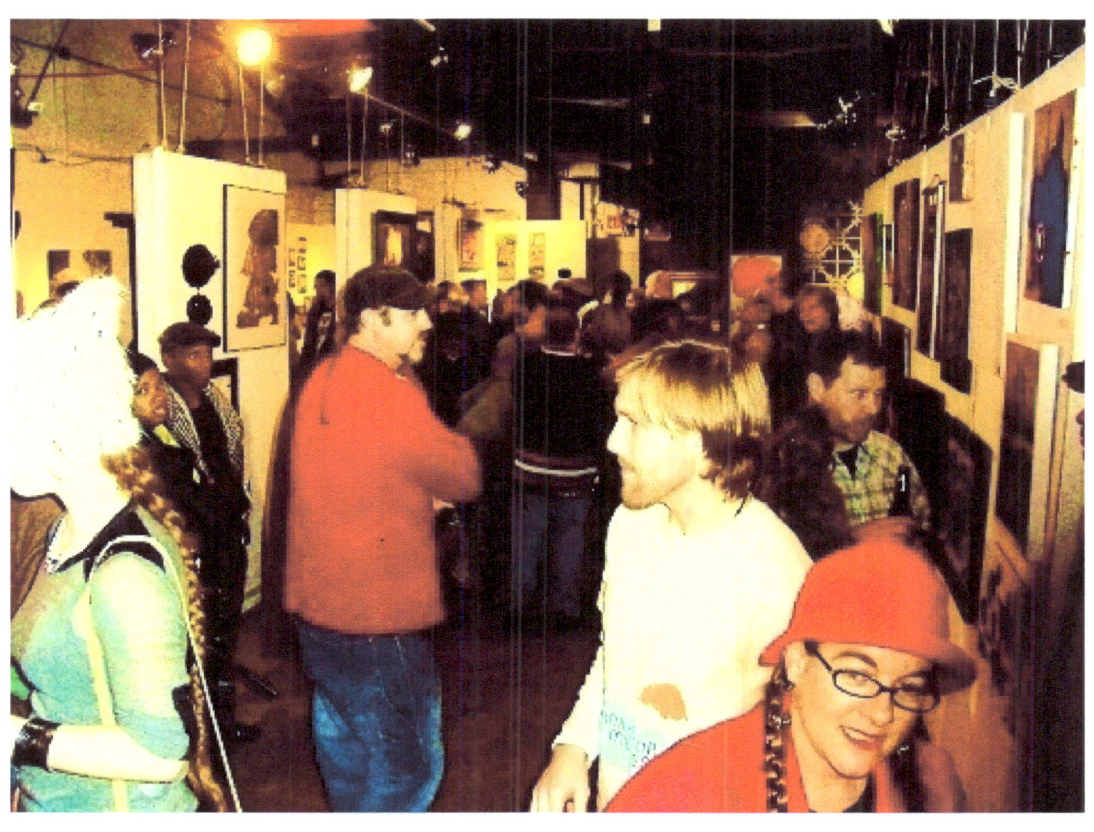

Artist and Crowd

**Pontoon Boat**

Hendersonville, Tennessee

Old Hickory Lake

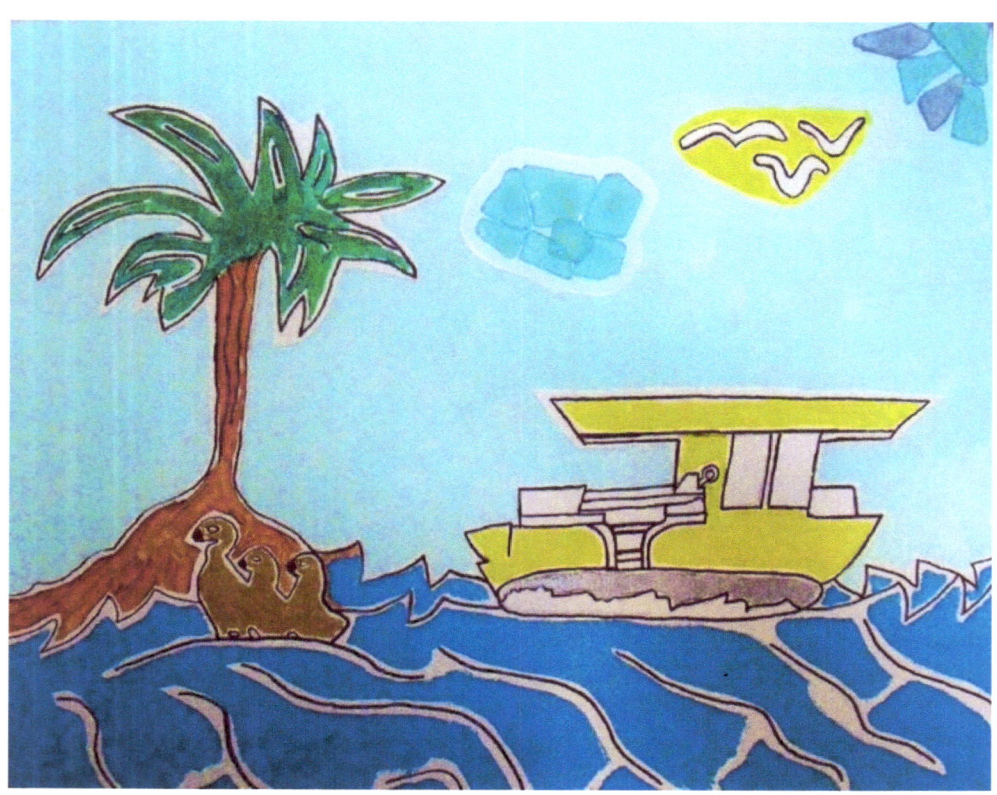

Acrylics and Pen

**Liberace - Peacock**

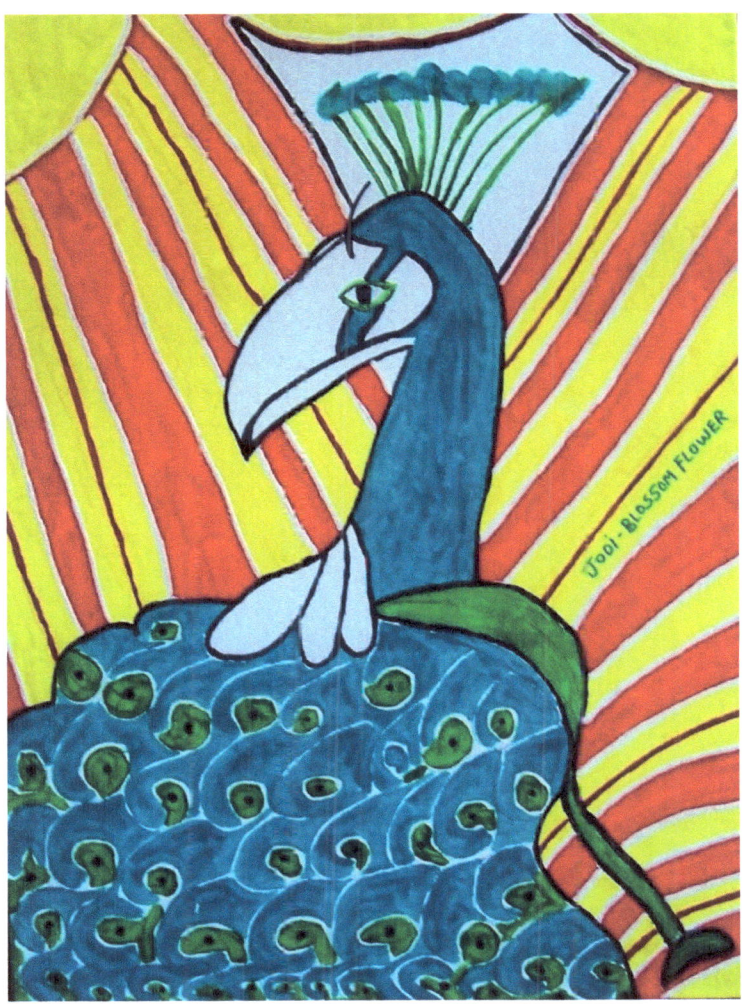

Acrylics, Watercolors and Pen

# Eagle - Flying Free

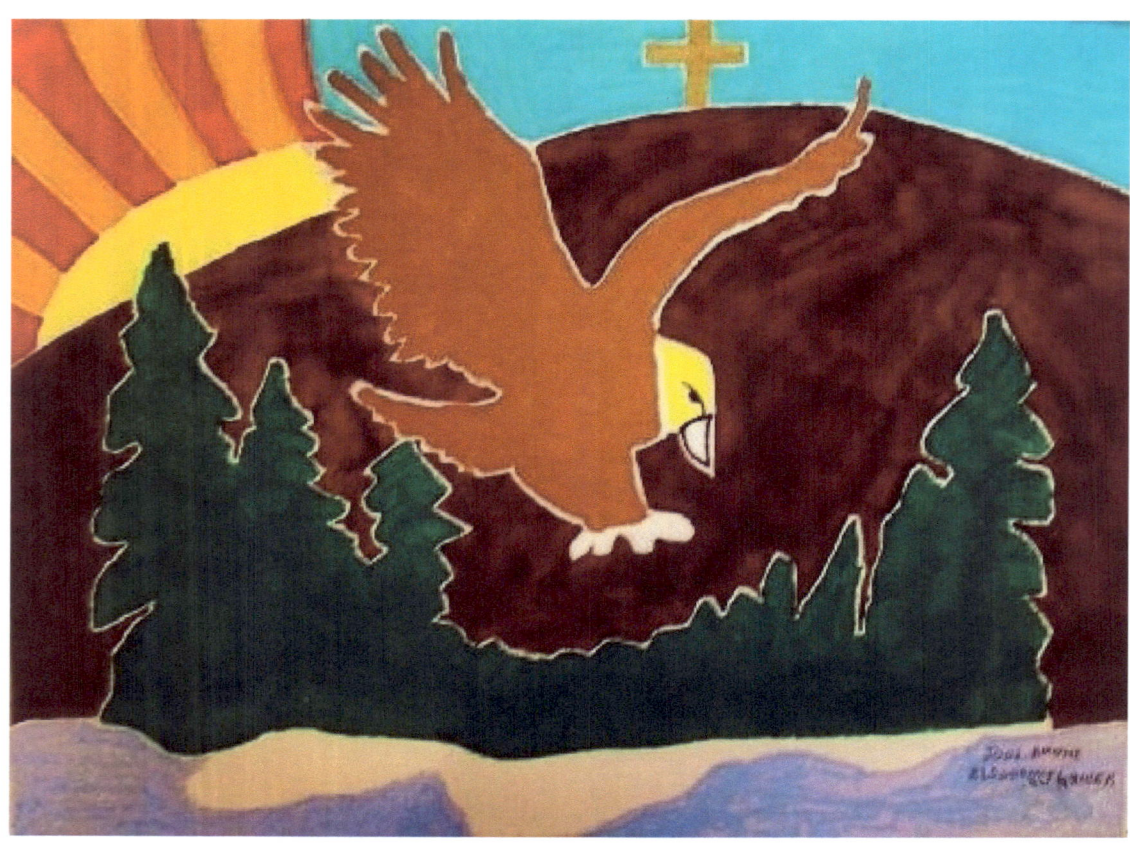

Acrylics and Watercolors

# Wine and Fruit

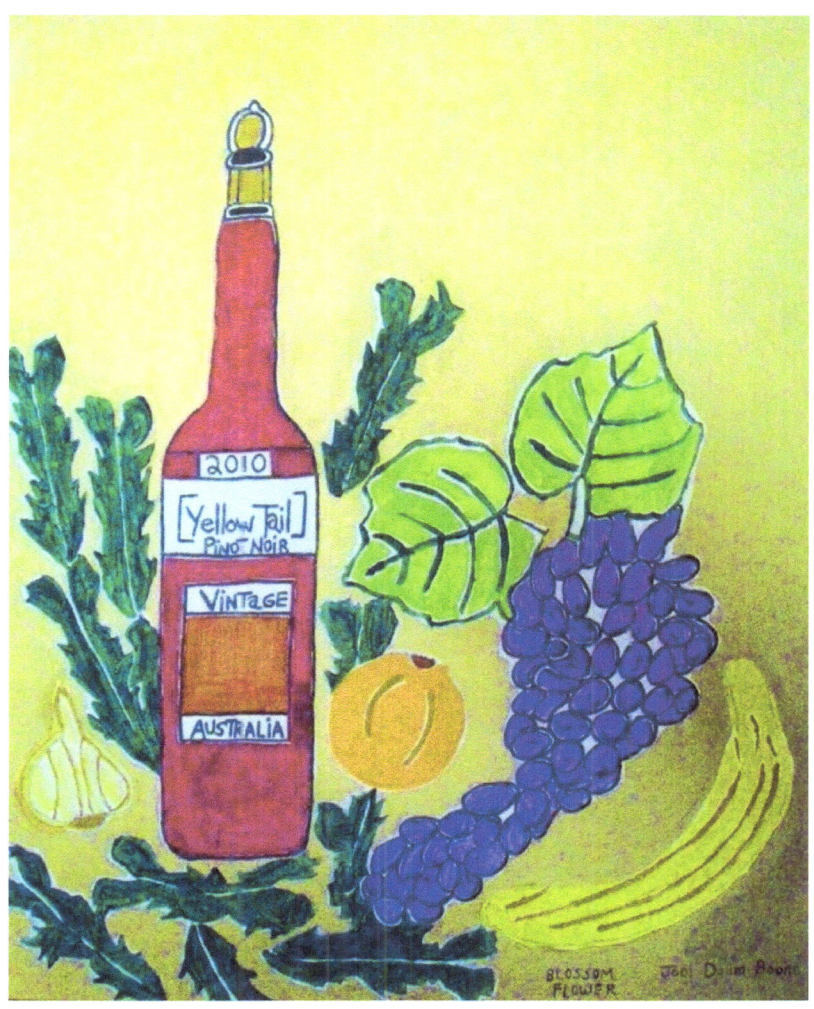

Acrylics and Pen

**Music Mania**

Gallatin, Tennessee

**Art Exhibit – 2010**

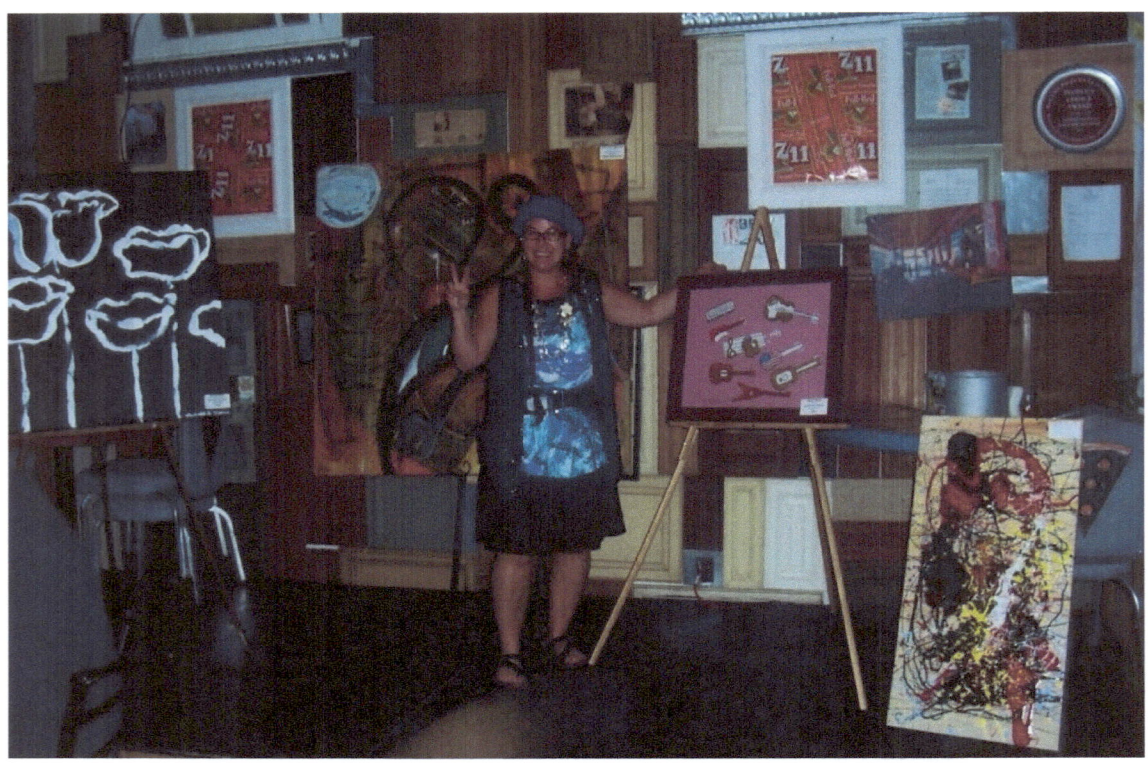

Acrylic – Music Mania – Instruments

# Music Mania

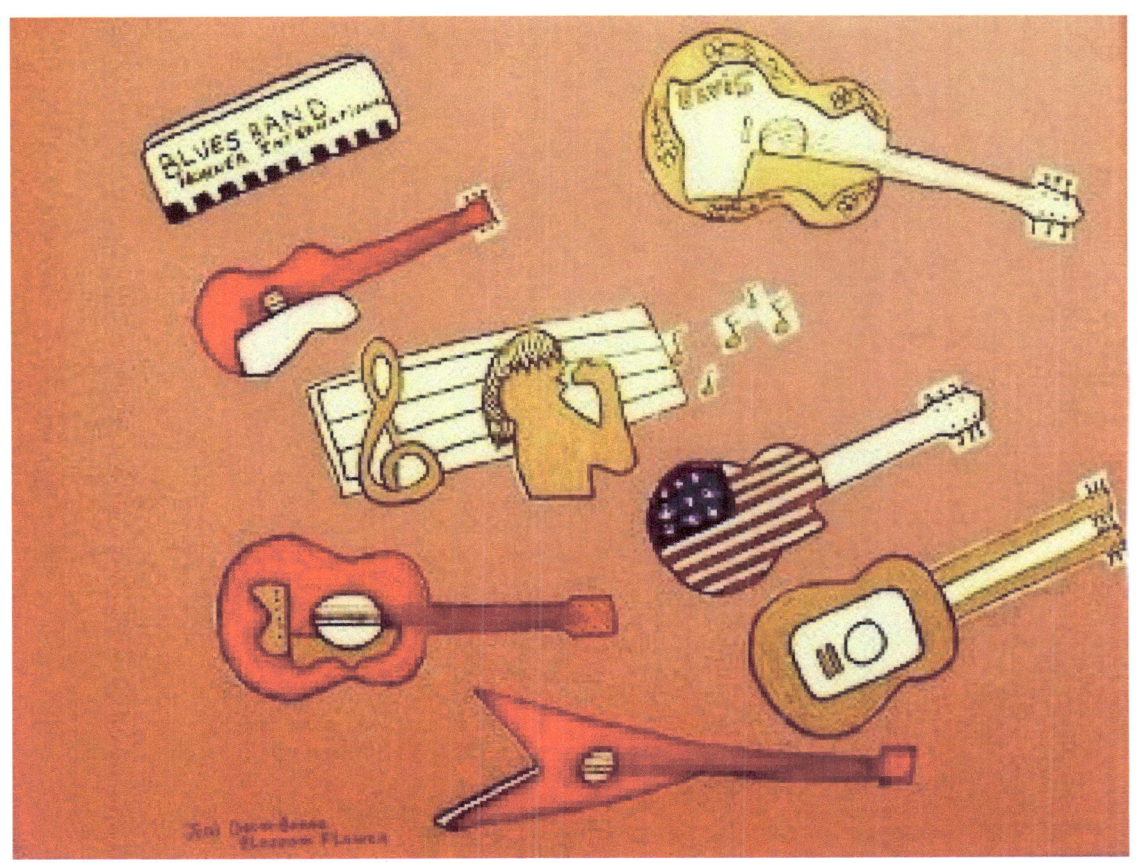

Acrylics and Pen

# Monthaven Art Society

Hendersonville, Tennessee

## Art Exhibit - Fall Season

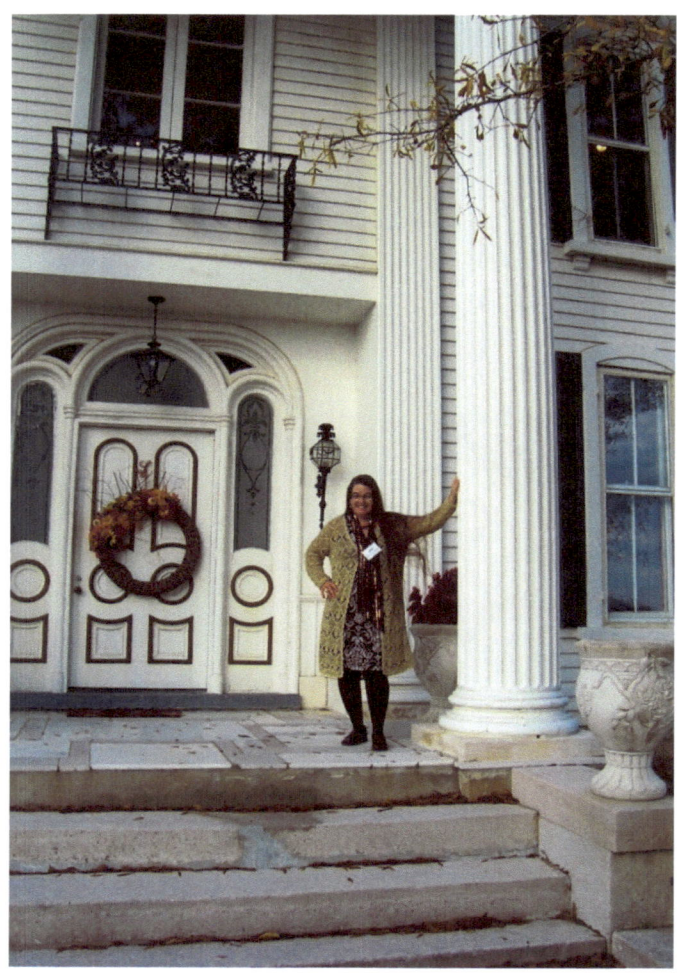

Held at the Historic Civil War Mansion

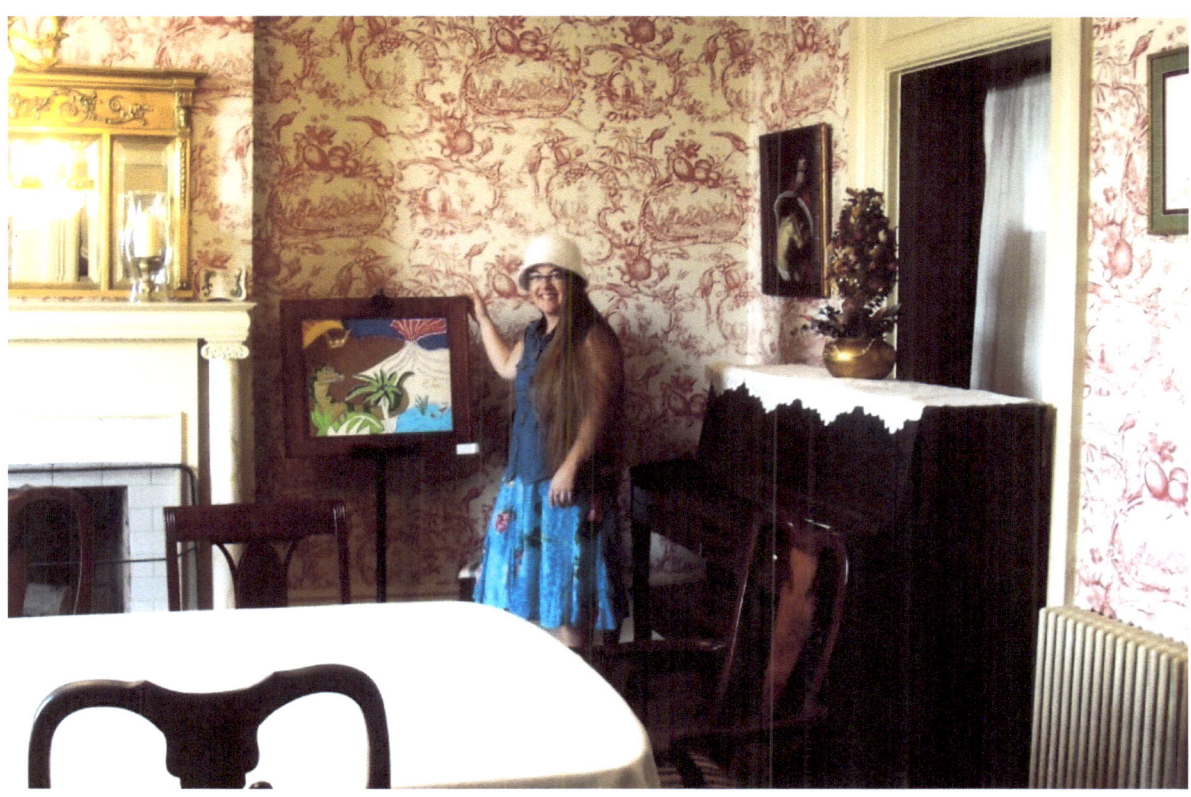

Painting in the Formal Dining Room

Title - Earth the Beginning of Time

Acrylics

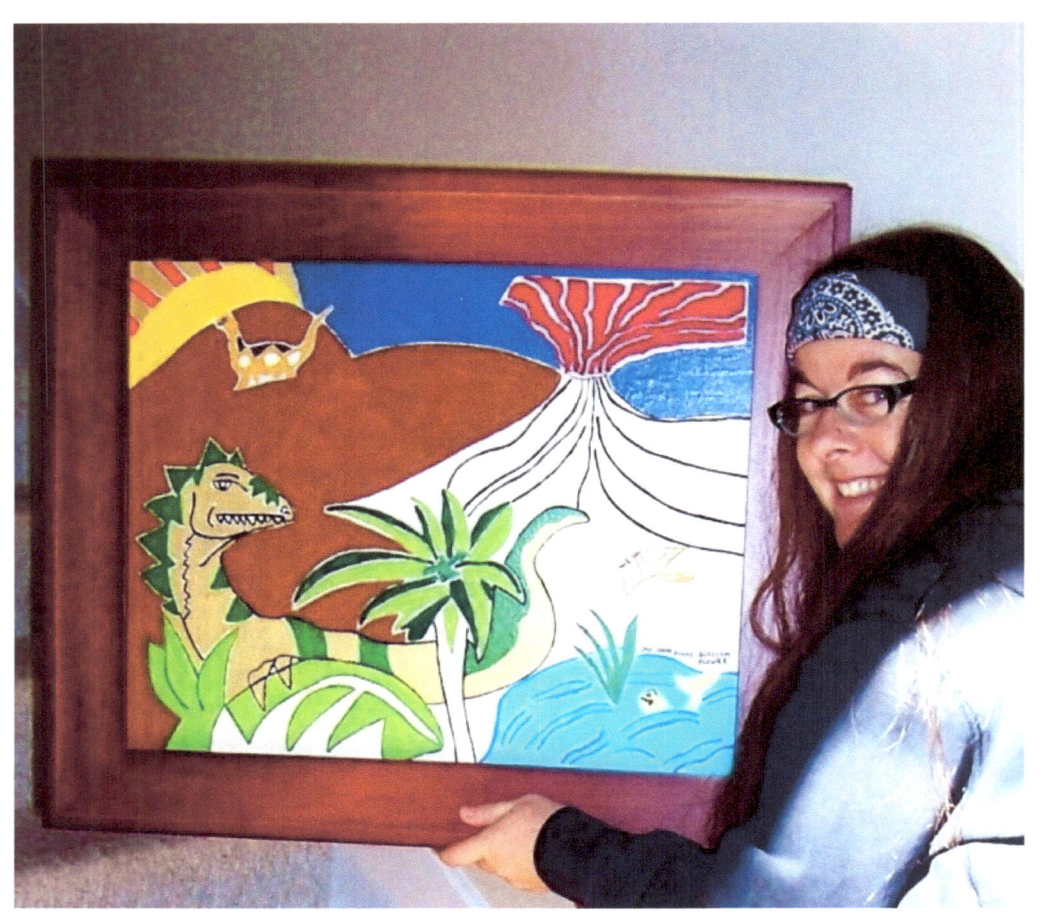

Artist – Vibrant Colors in Painting

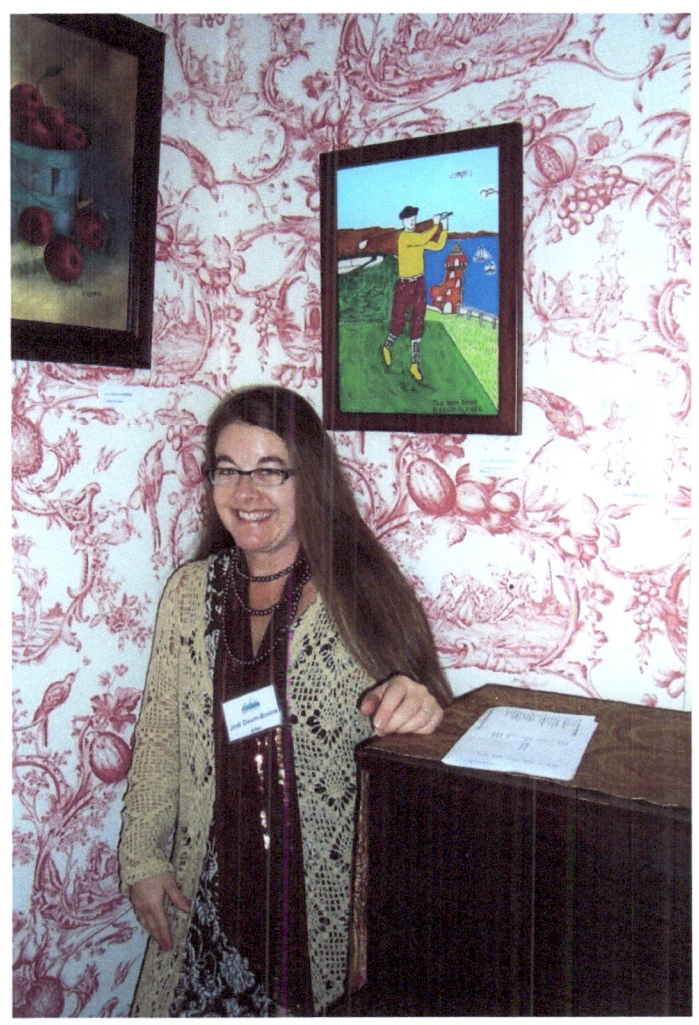

Jodi Daum Boone

Artist

Acrylic - The Pebble Beach Golfer

**World Peace**

Native American Indian-Horse Rider and Feathers

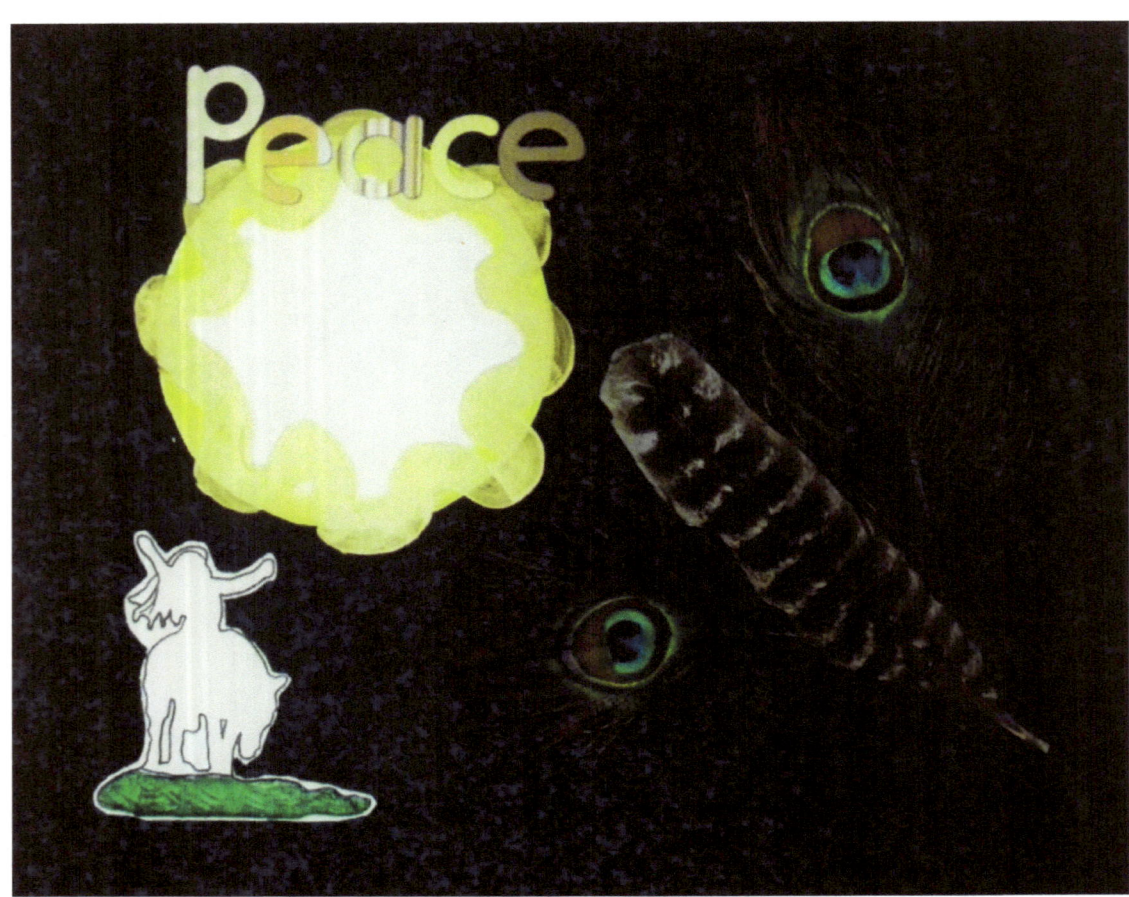

**Wired Coffee House**

Hendersonville, Tennessee

**Art Exhibit – 2010**

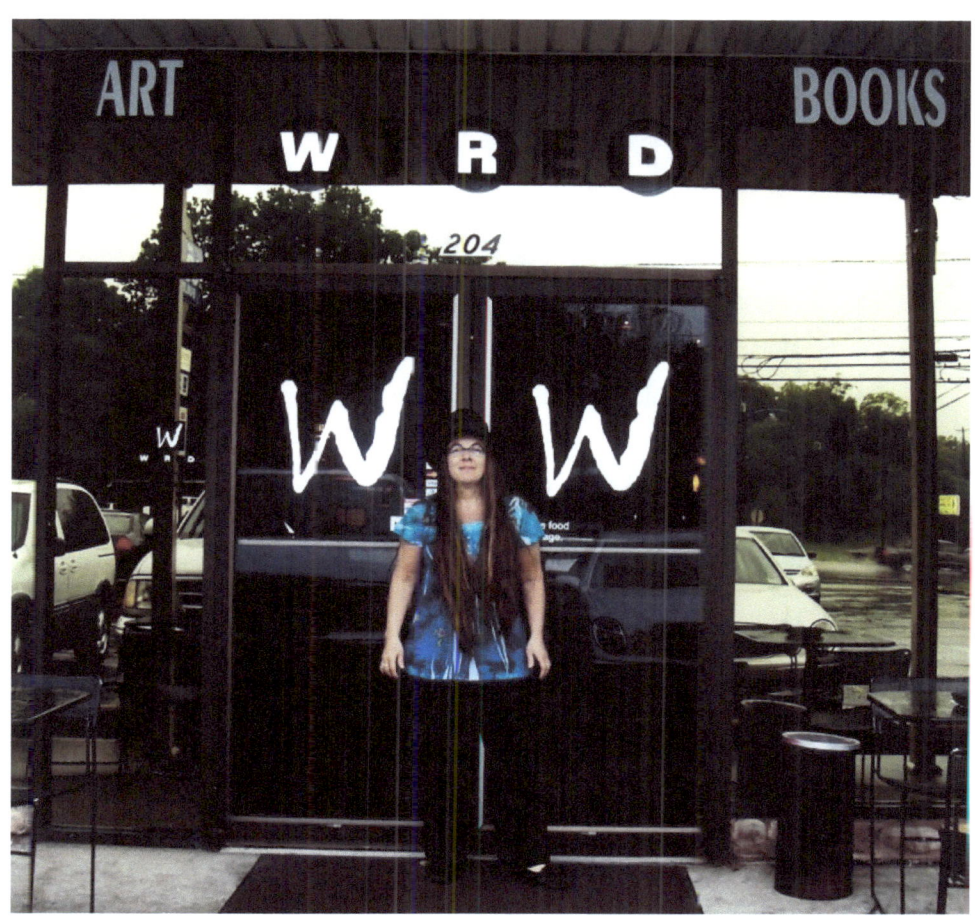

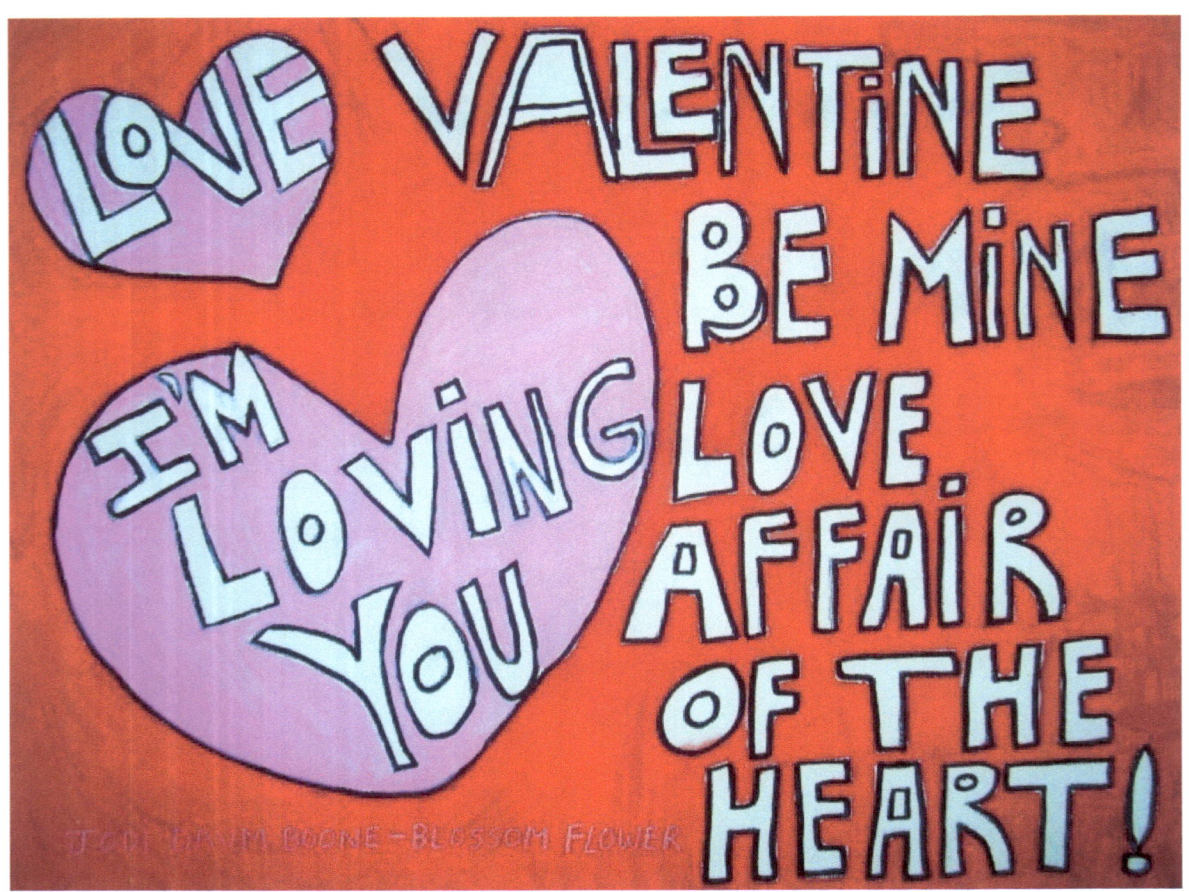

Acrylics

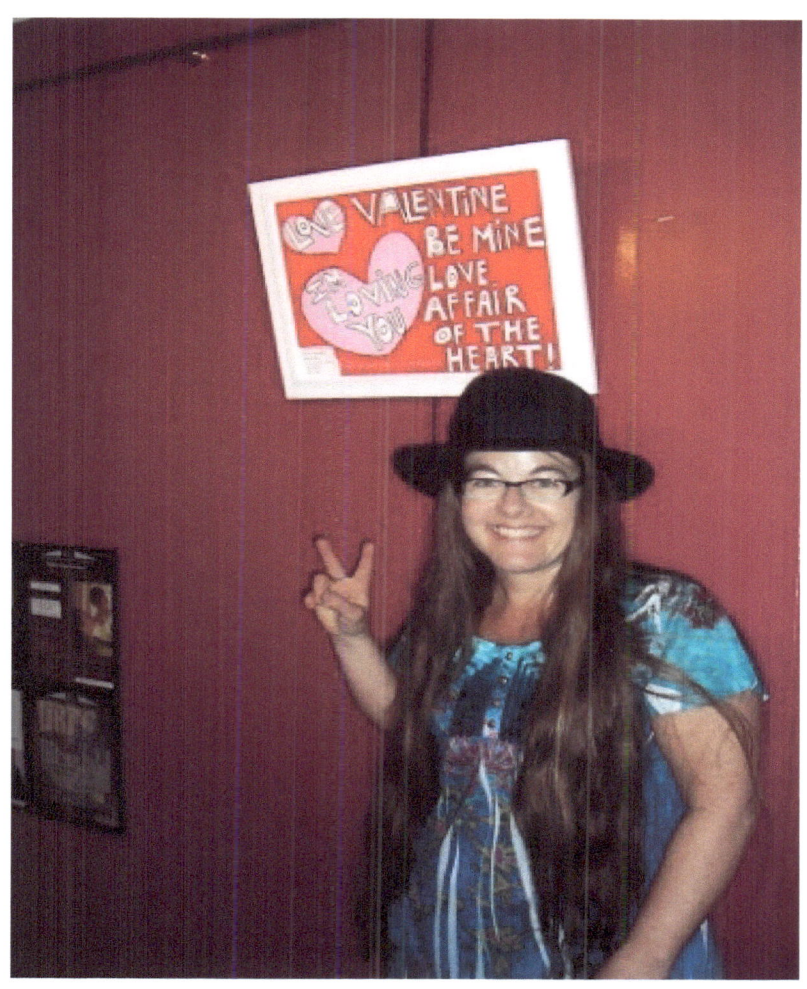

Peace and Love

# Ash Blonde

## Wine and Fruit

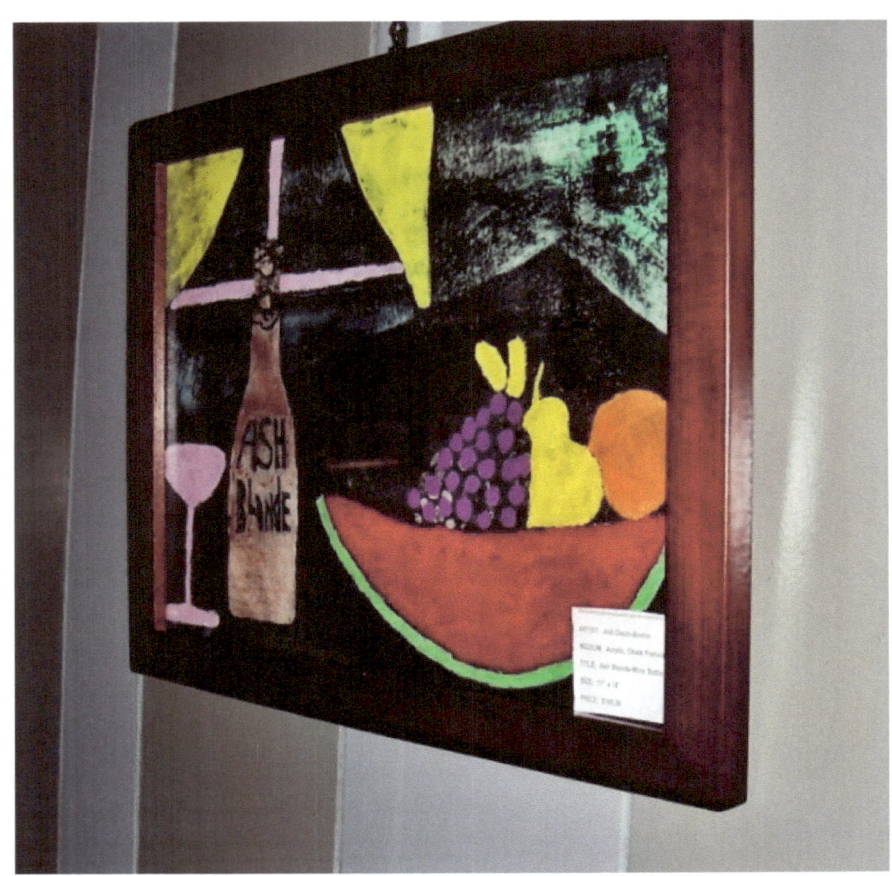

Acrylics and Pastels

# What is Hip!

## Bus

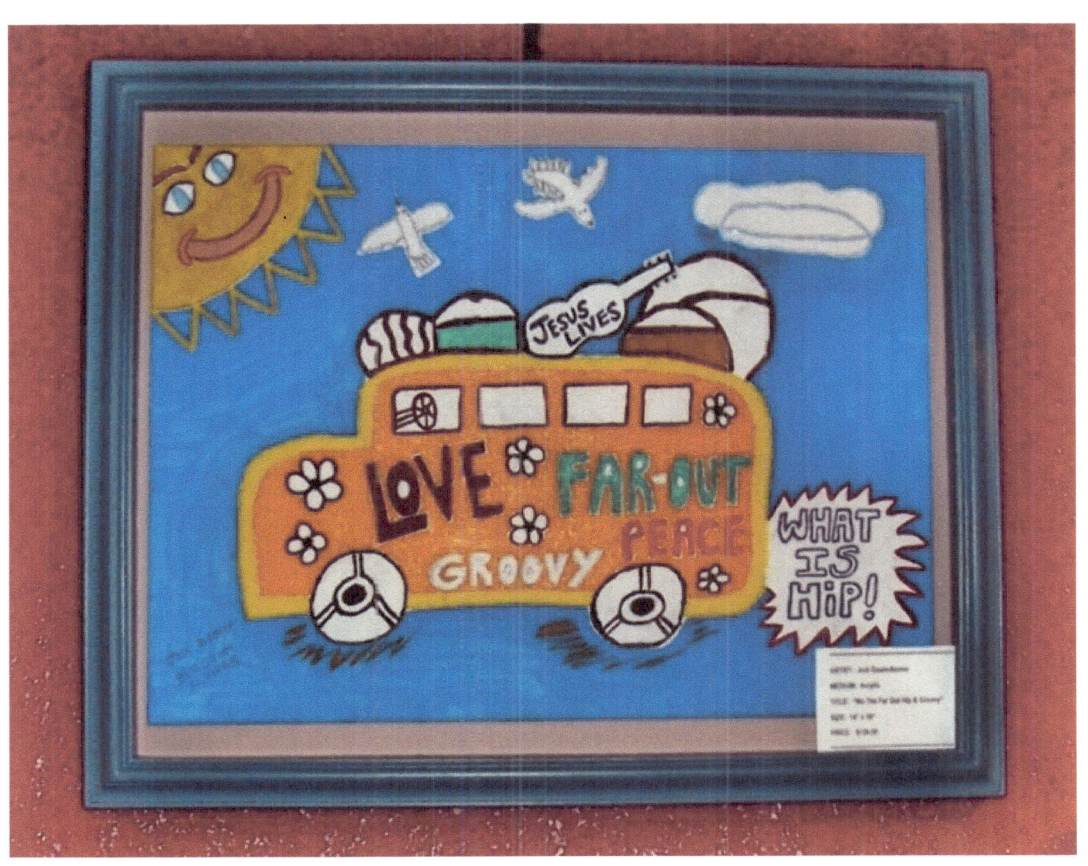

Acrylics

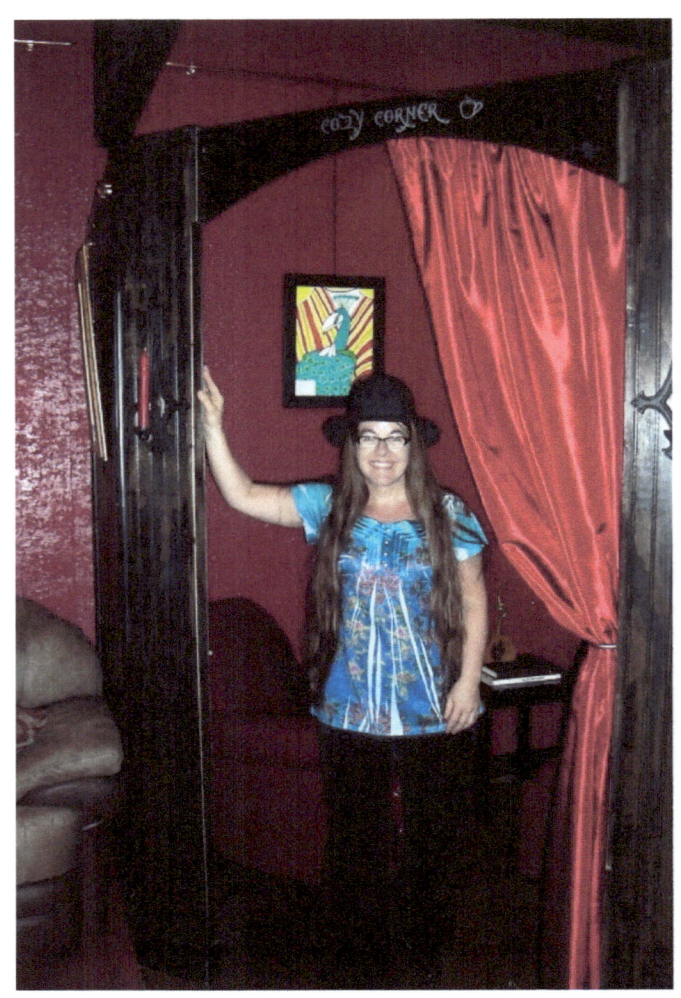

Freedom of Expression

**Blossom Flowers**

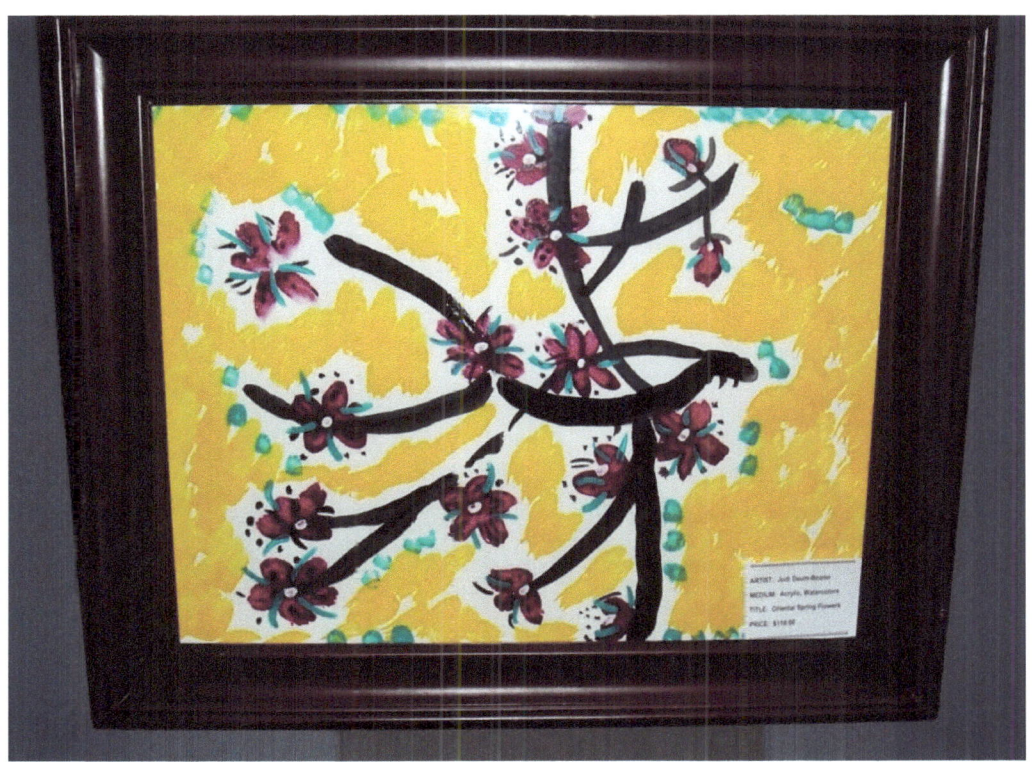

Acrylics

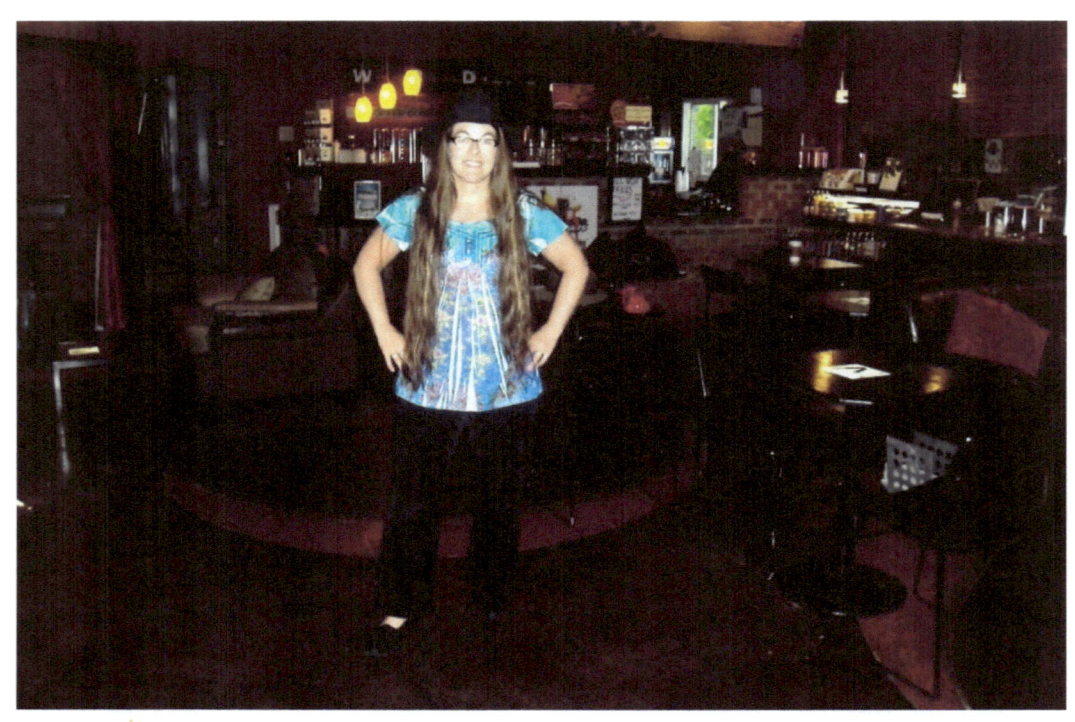

Art Exhibit - Coffee House

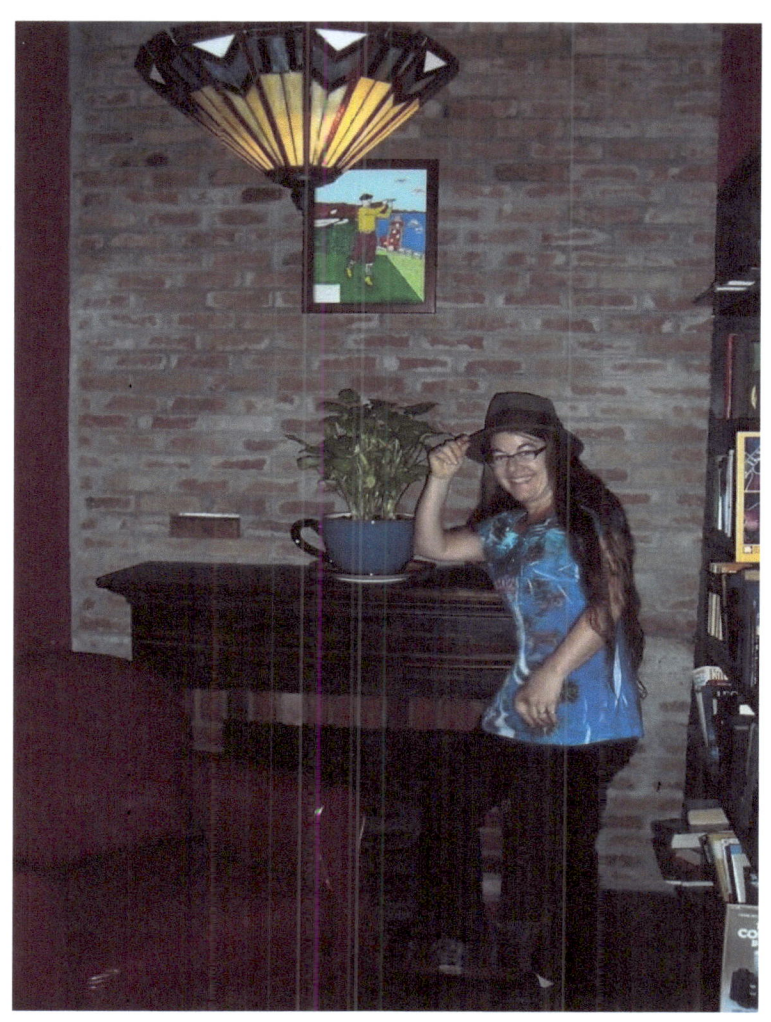

Cozy Fireplace

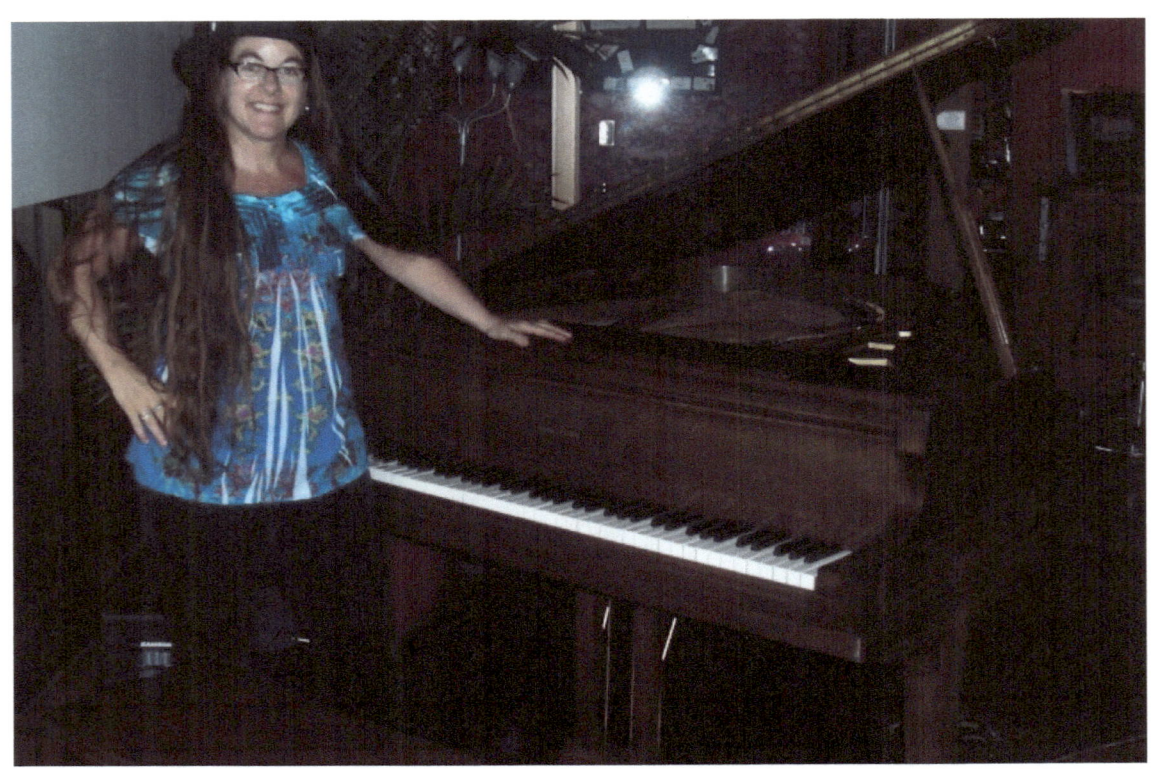

Piano Music

**Untitled Artist**

**Venue:  BB Kings Club**

Nashville, Tennessee

Art Exhibit – 2010

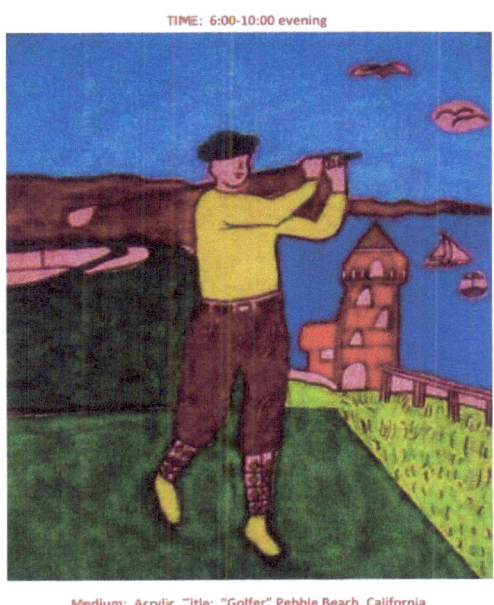

"Art Exhibit"  2010

ARTIST: Jodi Daum-Boone

VENUE:  BB Kings Club

SHOW:  MOJO – "Untitled Artist" - Over 100 Artist)

ADDRESS:  152  2$^{nd}$ Avenue North

LOCATION:  Nashville, Tennessee

TIME:  6:00-10:00 evening

Medium:  Acrylic, Title: "Golfer" Pebble Beach, California

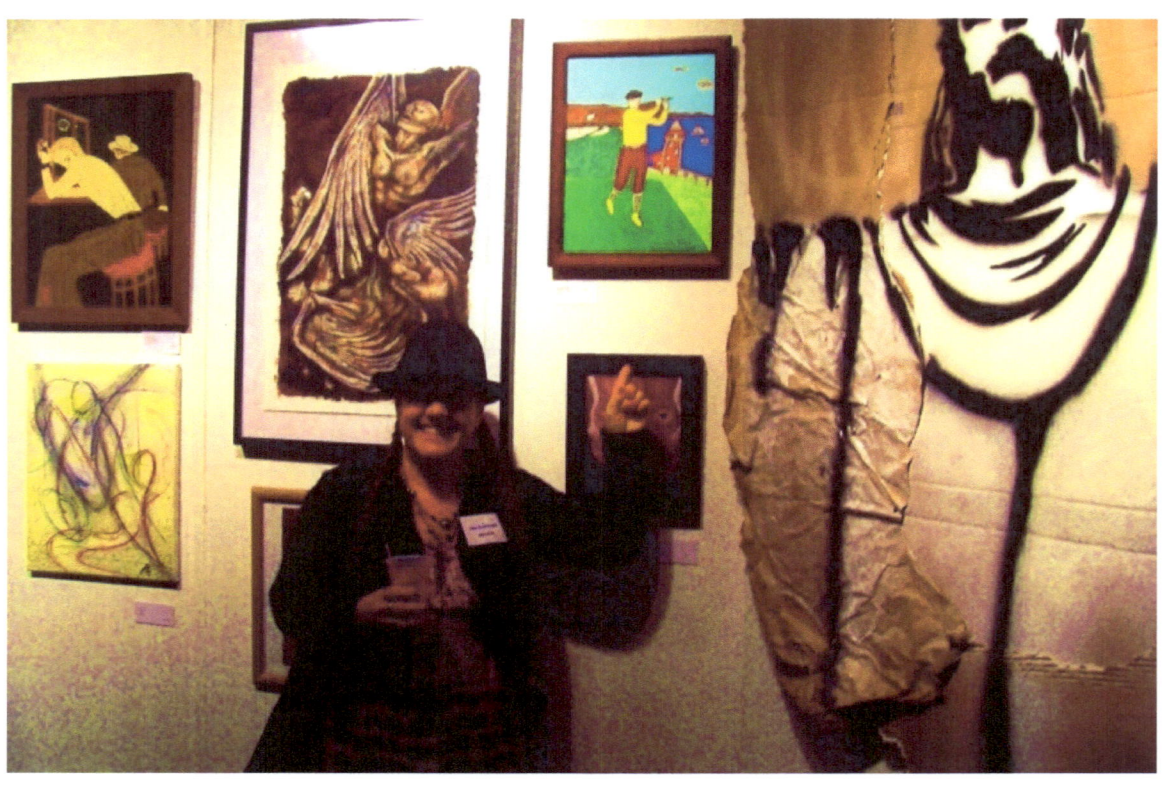

Painting of Golfer

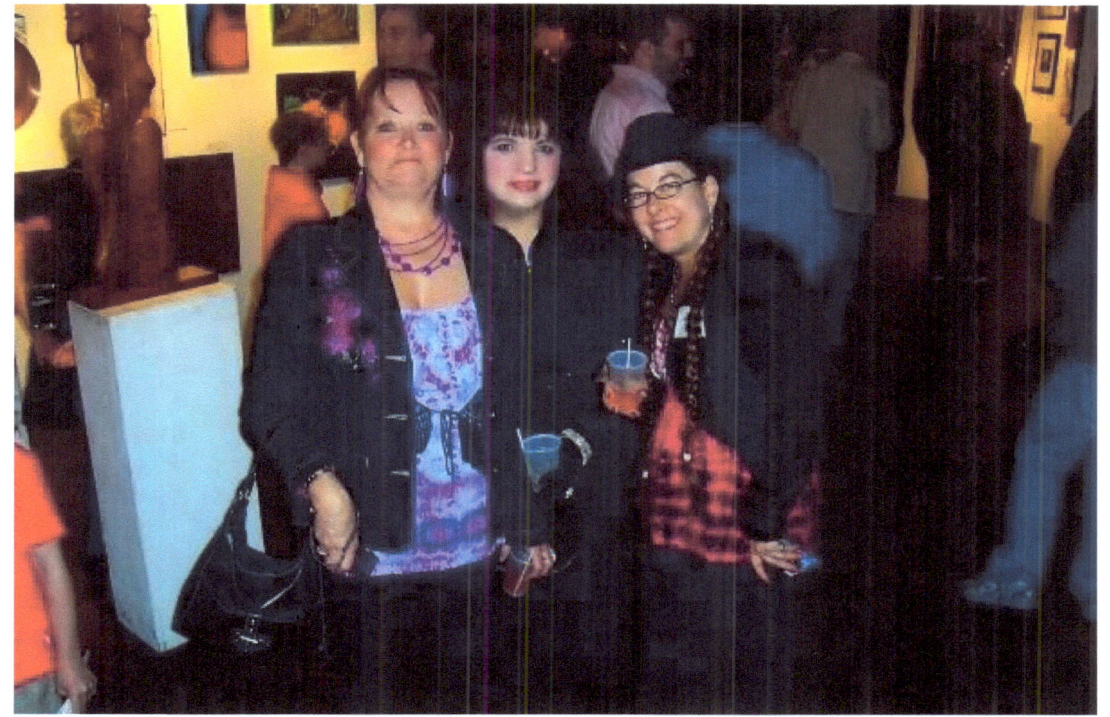

Artist

Debbie Gilbert, Peggy Leyva Conley and Jodi Daum Boone

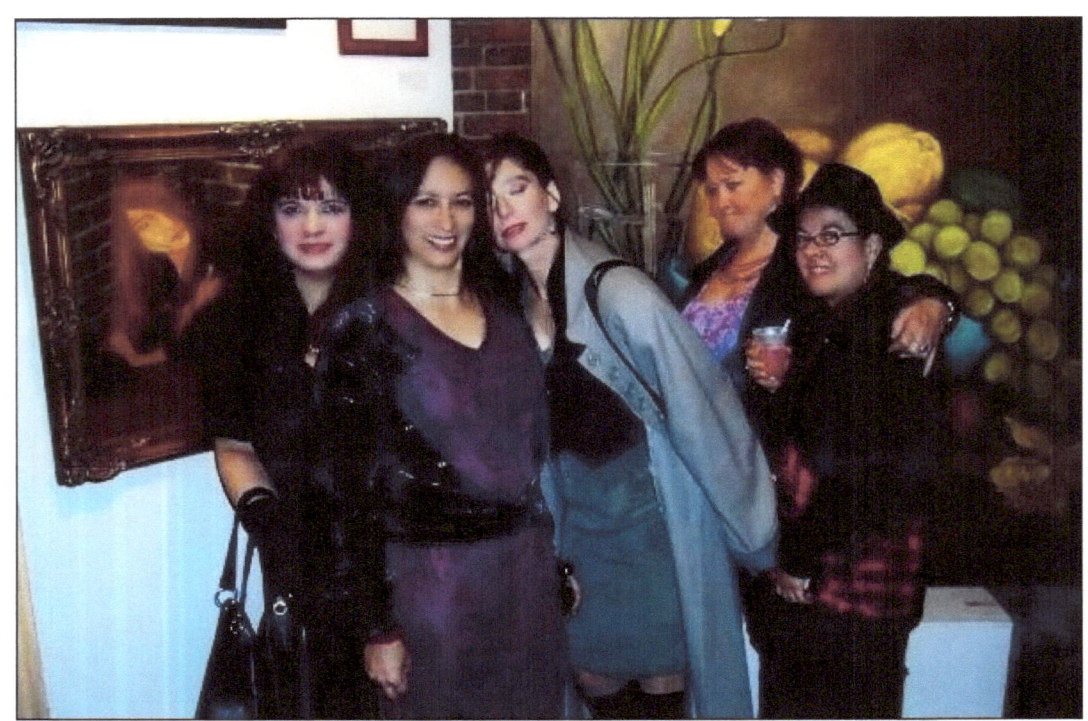

Artist and Musicians – Nashville, Tennessee


Left:  Peggy Leyva Conley, Wil Maring, Chris Daniex,

Debbie Gilbert and Jodi Daum Boone

**Monthaven Art Society**

**Venue - Comer Mansion**

Gallatin, Tennessee

Art Exhibit – Summer

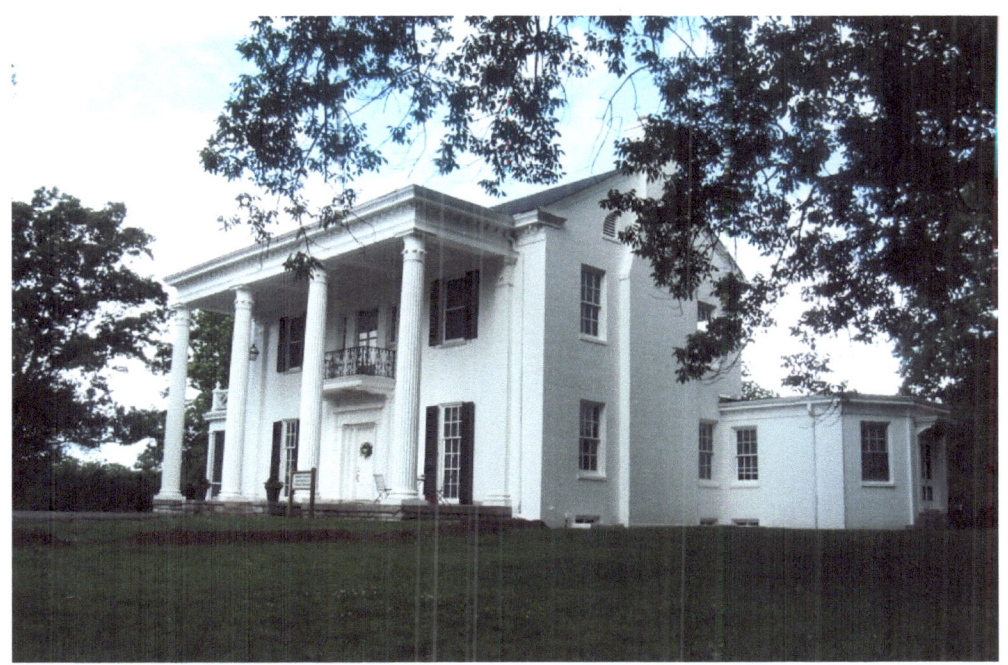

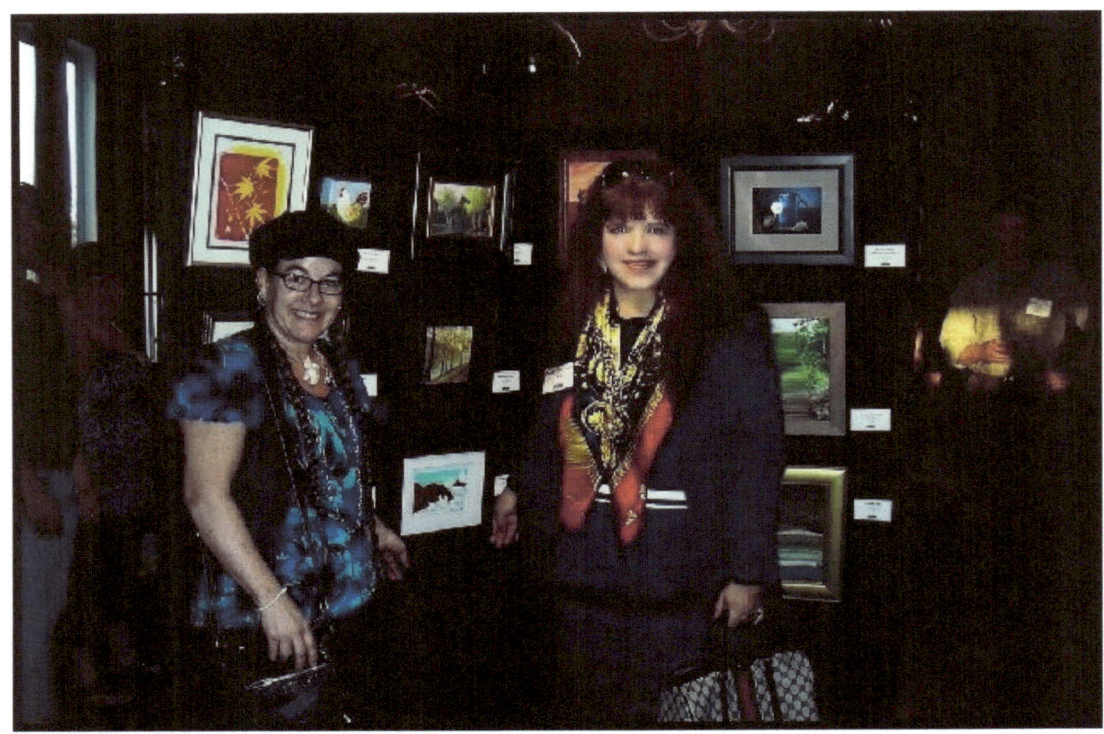

Artist

Left:  Jodi Daum Boone and Peggy Leyva Conley

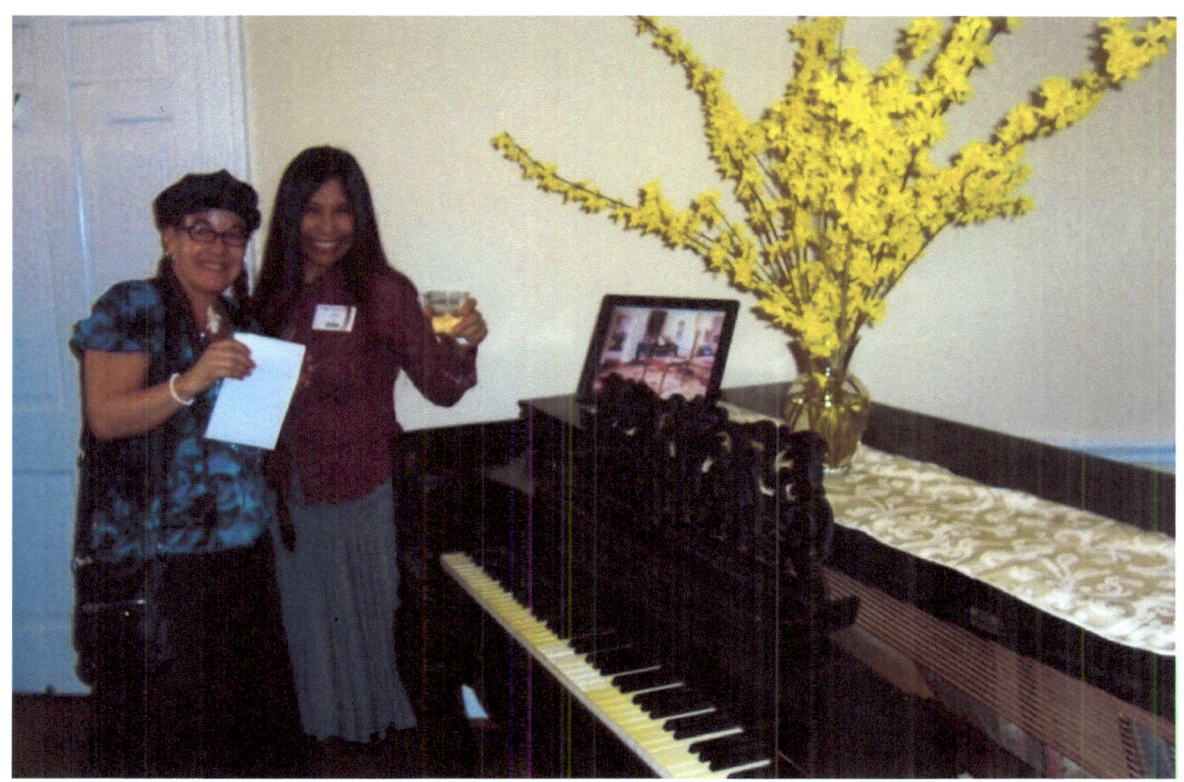

Artist


Left – Jodi Daum Boone and Tess

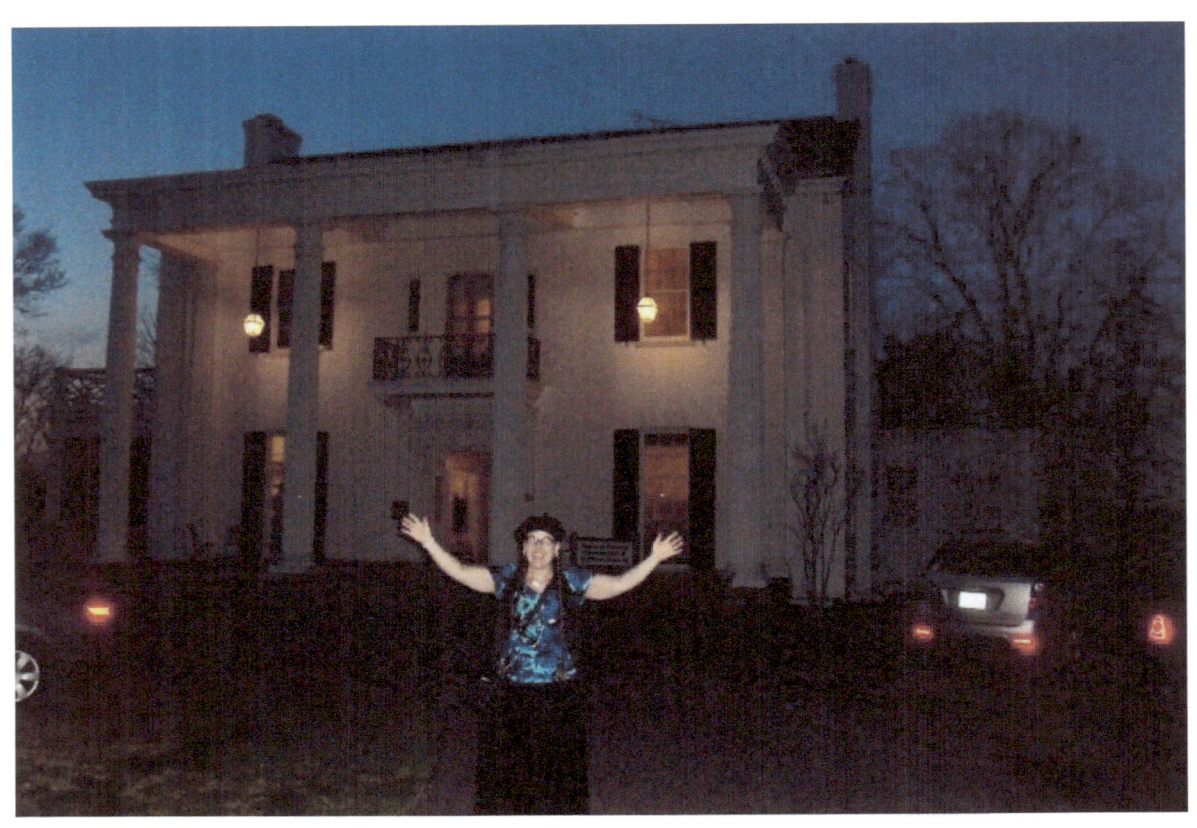

Comer Mansion – Jodi Daum Boone

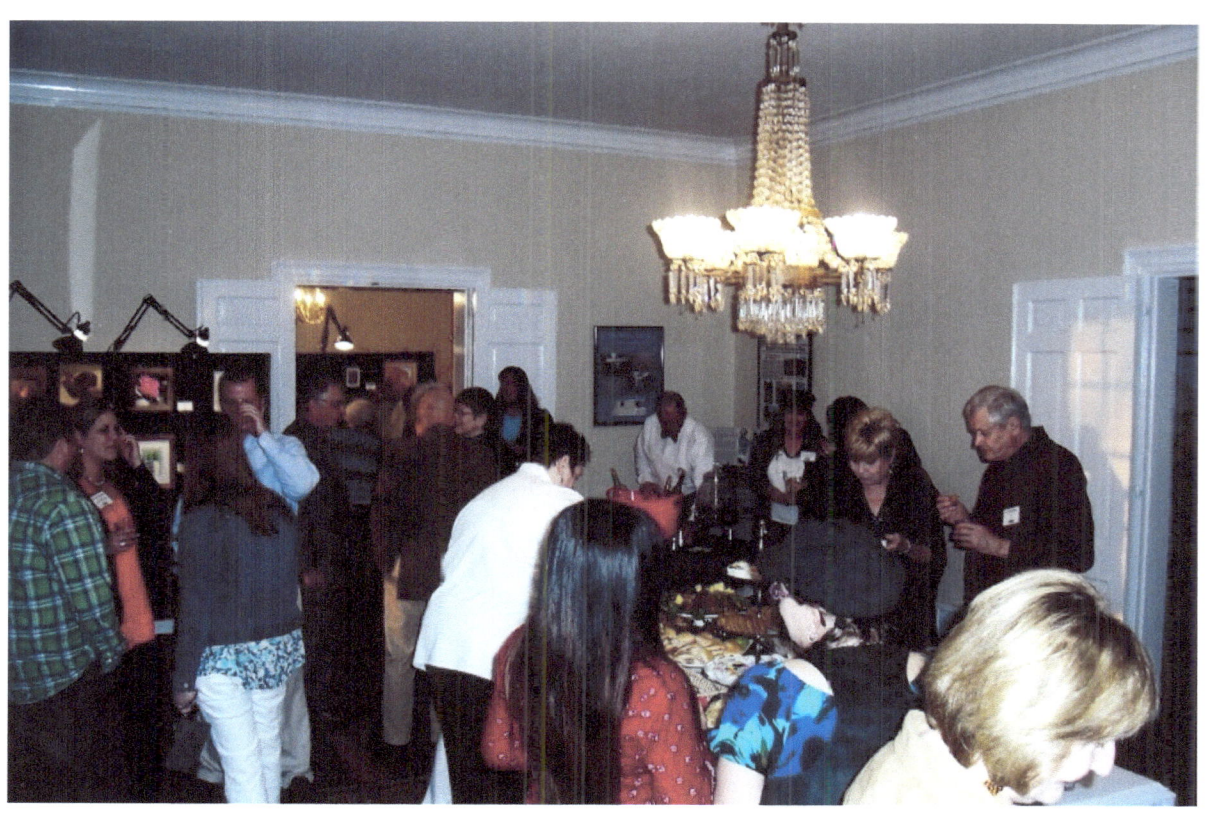

Artist and Guest

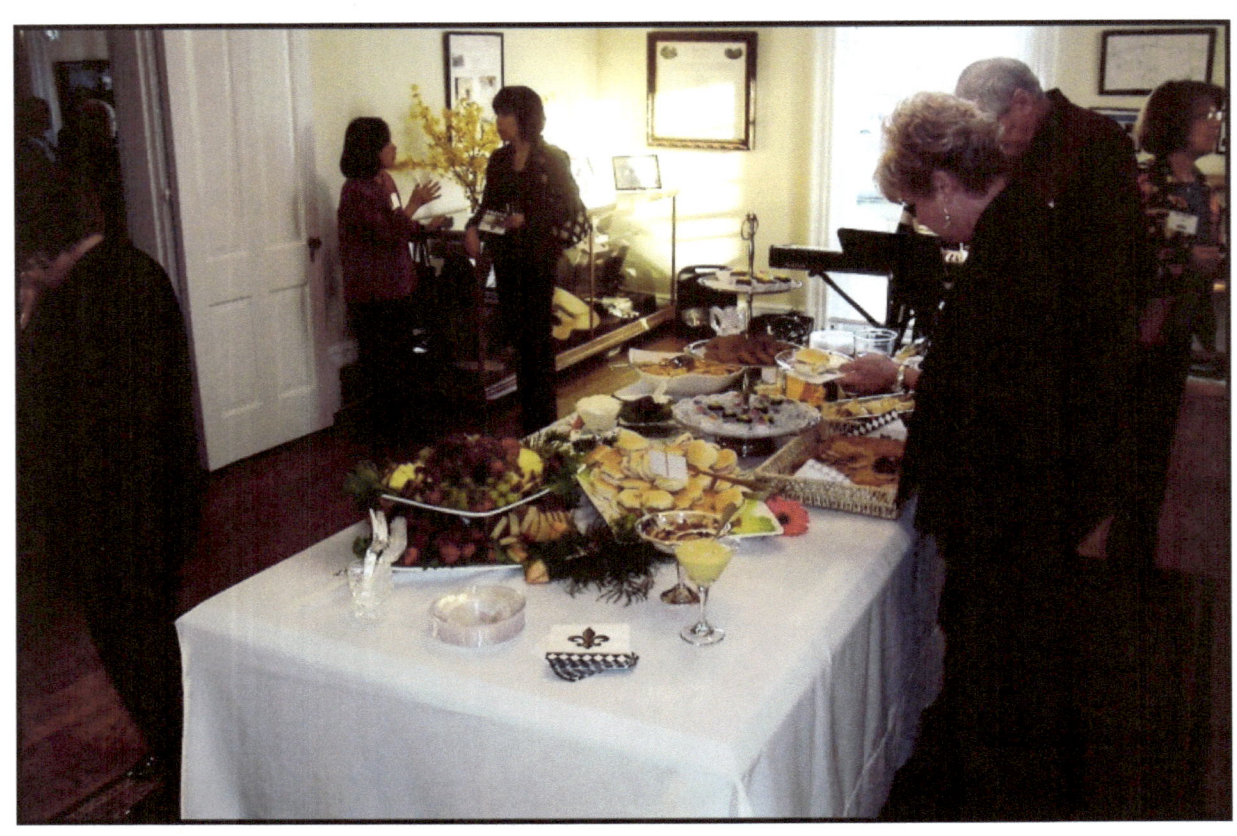

Buffet

**Untitled – Naked Carnival**

**Venue – Diamond Sound Studios**

Nashville, Tennessee

**Art Exhibit - 2008**

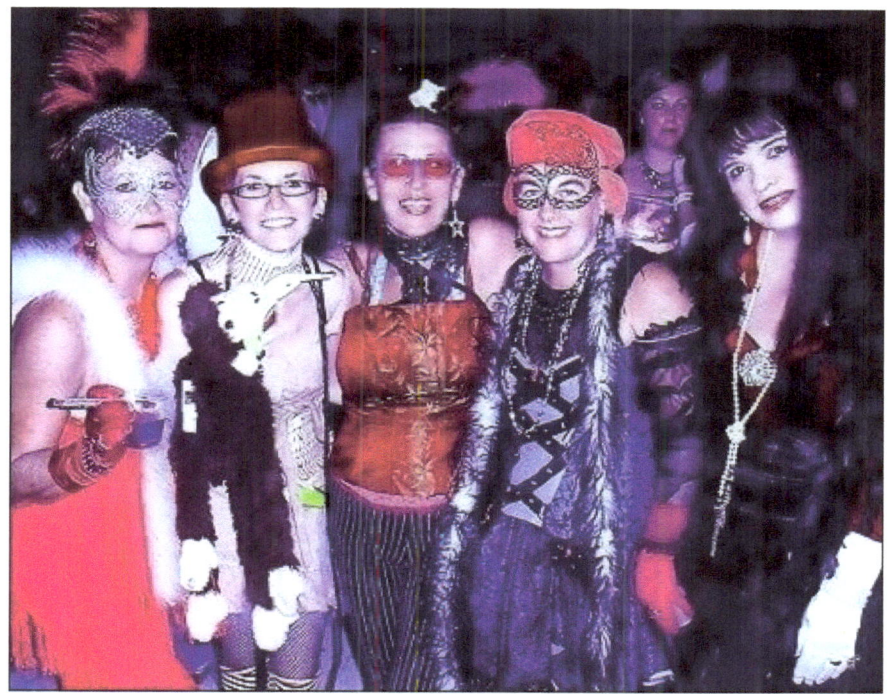

Left:  Debbie Gilbert, Samantha Callahan,

Von Derry, Jodi Daum Boone, Peggy Leyva Conley

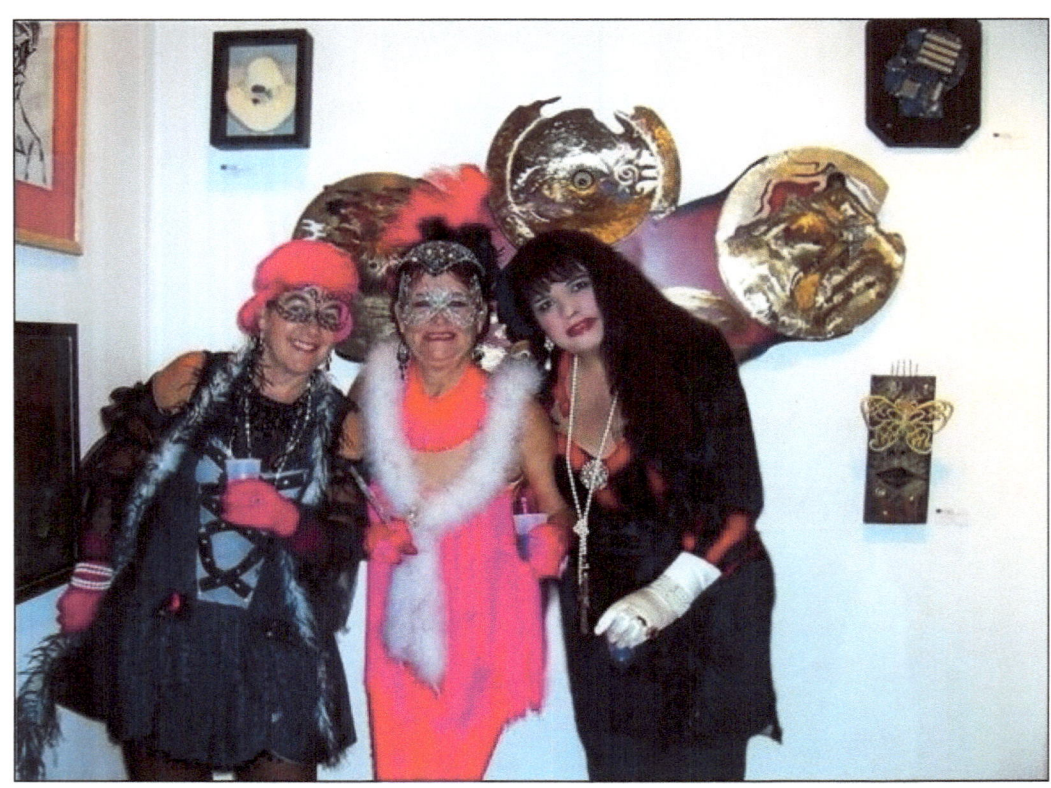

Left:  Jodi Daum Boone, Debbie Gilbert, Peggy Leyva Conley

**Untitled – The Island of Misfits**

Venue – Building

Madison, Tennessee

**Art Exhibit – Winter**

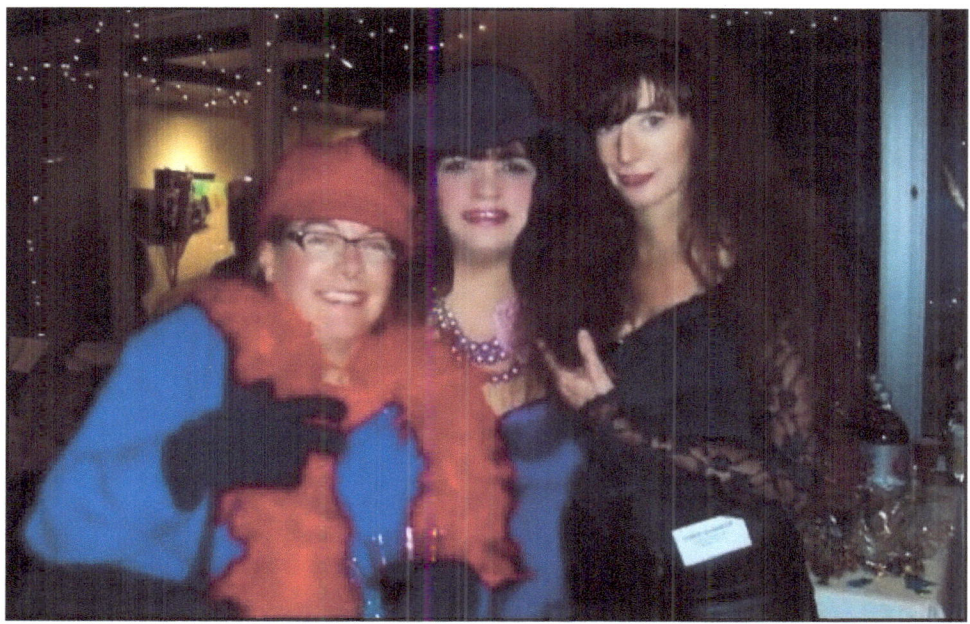

Left:  Jodi Daum Boone, Peggy Leyva Conley, Chris Daniecx

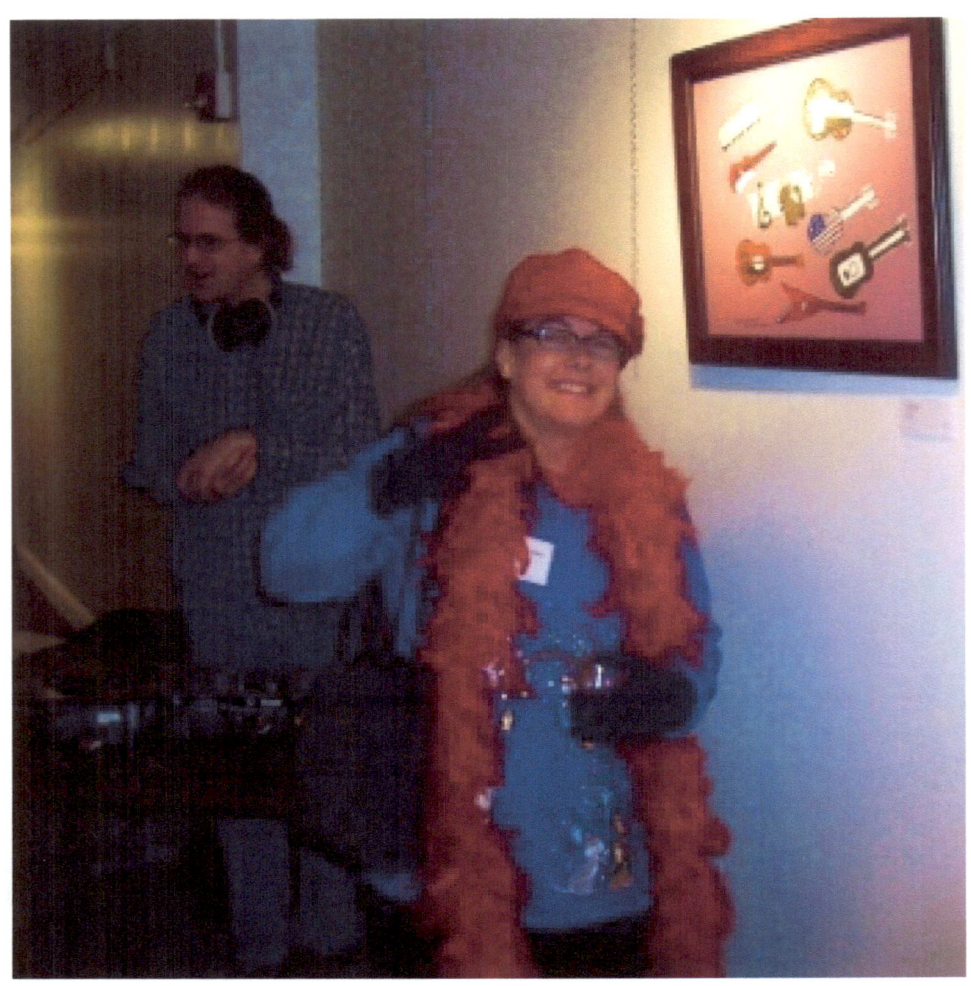

Peace and Love


Holiday Cheers !

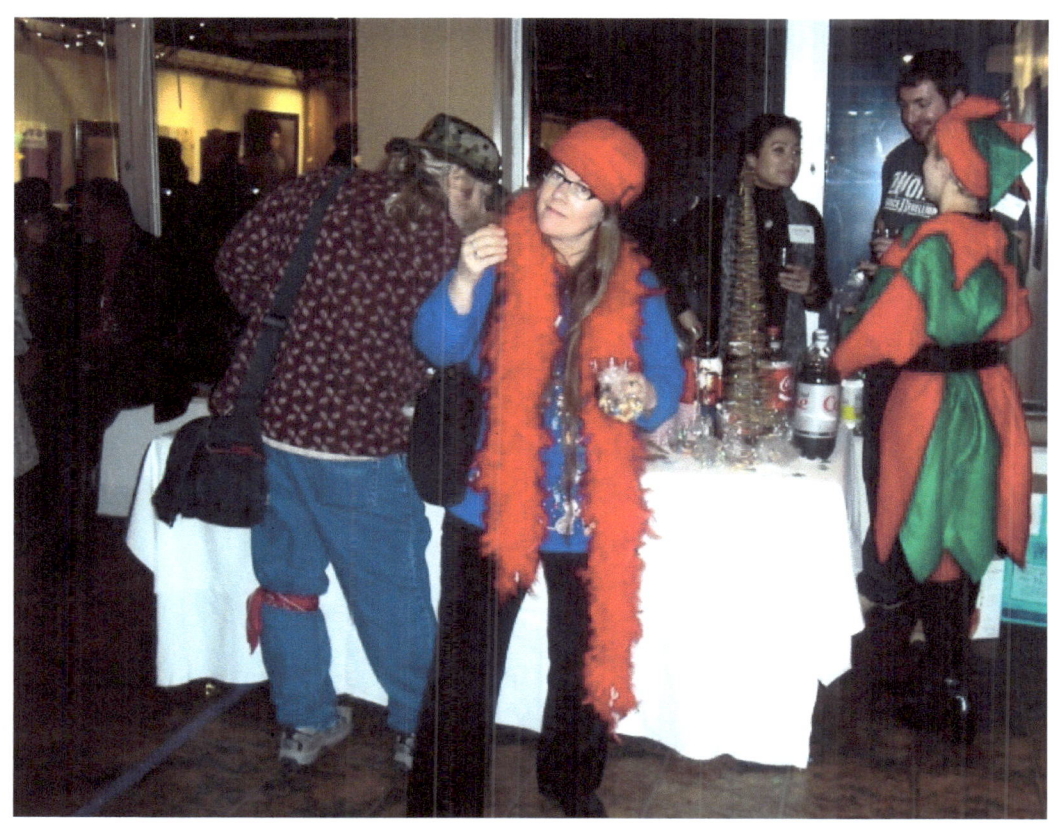

Artist – Cheers!

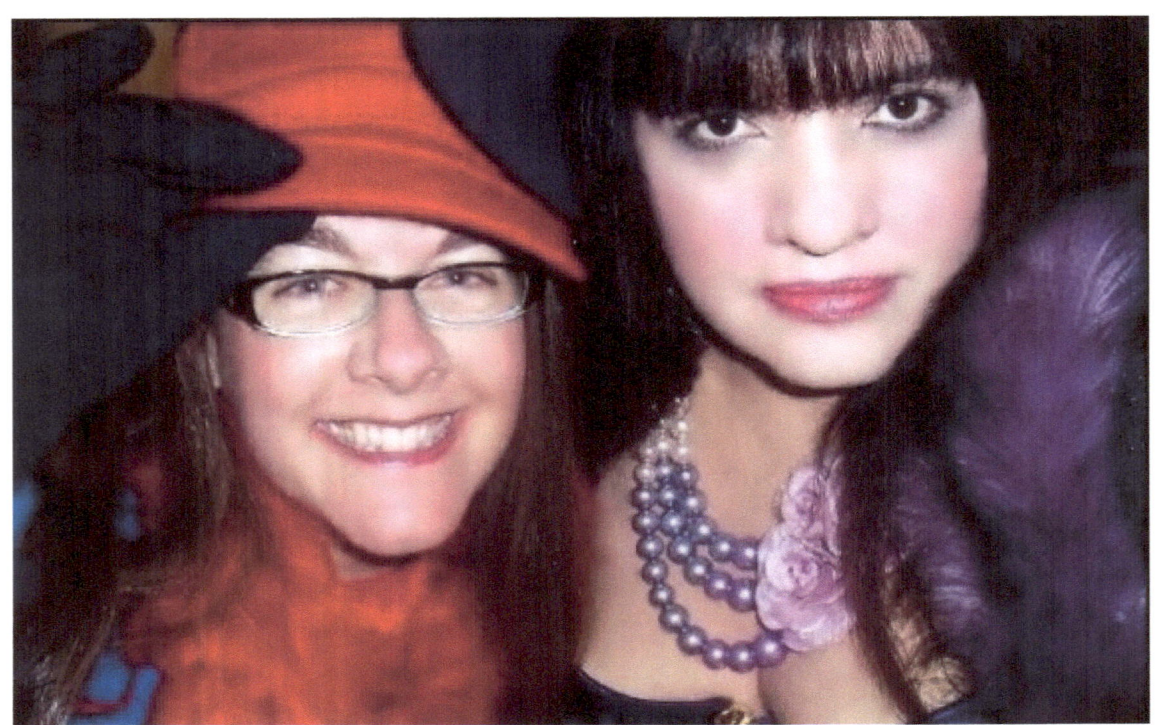

Artist

Jodi Daum Boone and Peggy Leyva Conley

**Untitled Artist**

**Venue – East Gallery**

Nashville, Tennessee

**Art Exhibit – Winter 2013**

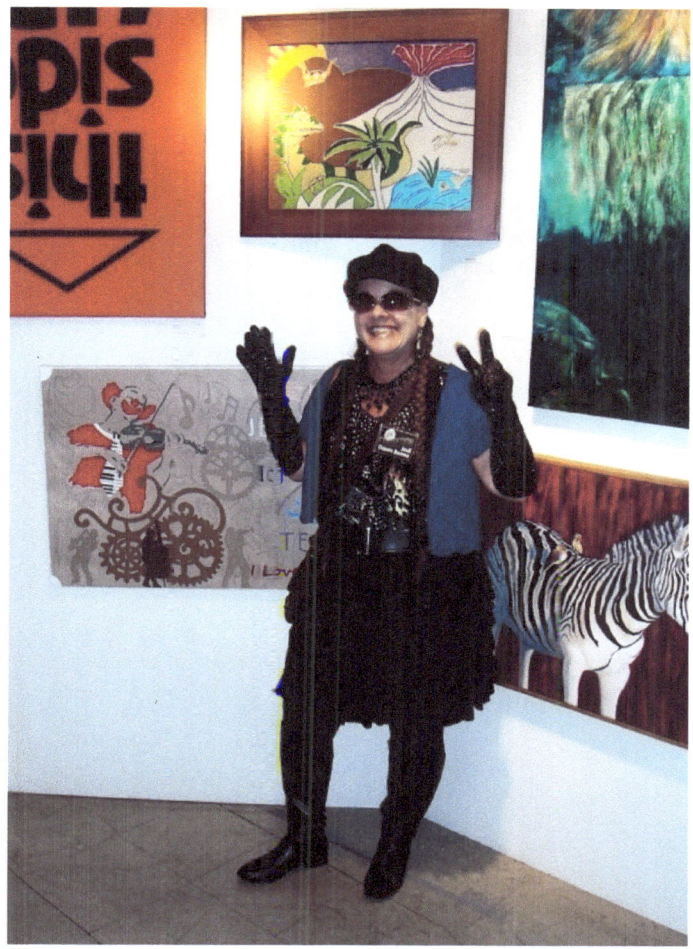

Peace and Love!

Keep Smiling and Painting

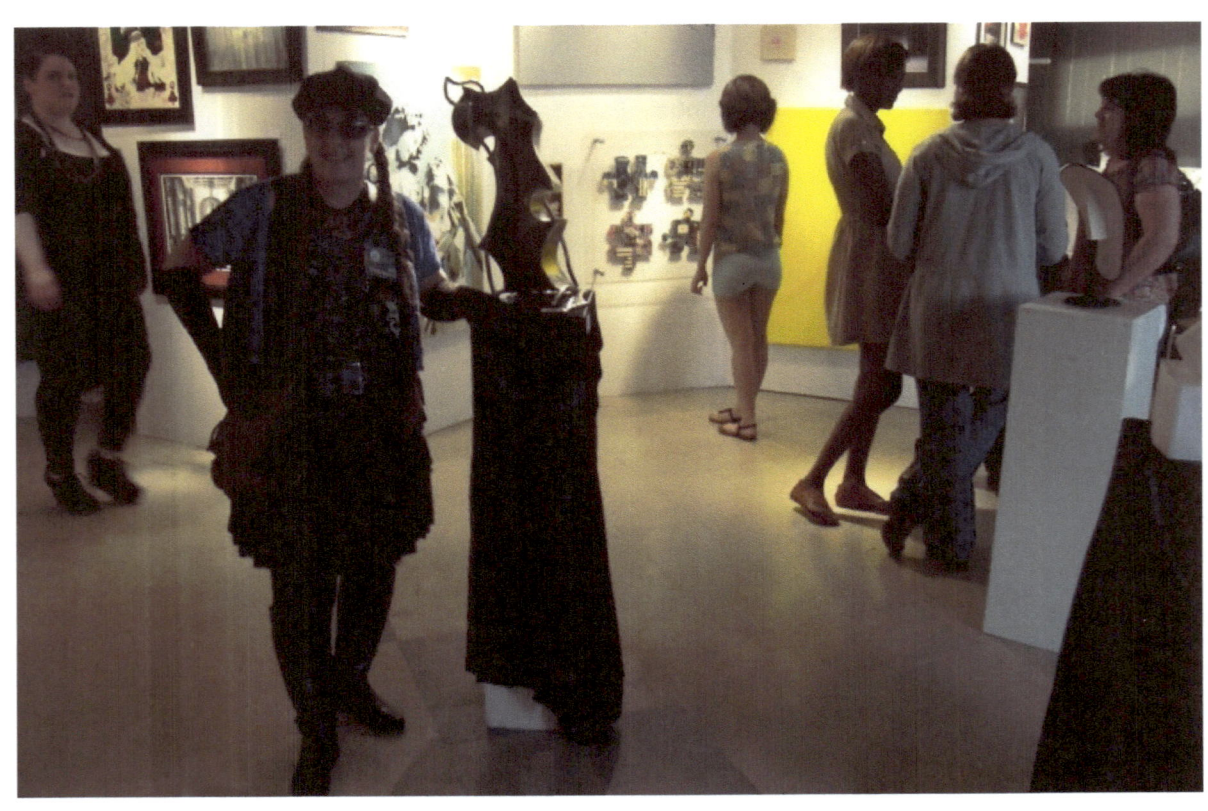

Art Show – Jodi Daum Boone and Crowd

## Literary Published Works

Jodi Daum Boone

### Books

**Paintings in Style**
Art Exhibits – Published 2016

**Adventures of the Human Spirit**
Poetry – Published 2016

**Natures Thoughts in Life**
Poetry – Published 2016

**Memories of Yesterday**
Poetry – Published 2016

**Walking in Celebration of Songwriting...Lyrics of Real Life**
Poetry – Published 2016

### Discography – Music

**CD-Peaceful Awakening**
Songs-Vocals (Folk, Country, Jazz) – Published 2014

**Available on International Distribution**

www.ingramcontent.com/pod-product-compliance
Lightning Source LLC
Chambersburg PA
CBHW050859180526
45159CB00007B/2733